COPING BETTER WITH CHRONIC FATIGUE SYNDROME/MYALGIC ENCEPHALOMYELITIS

The Self-help Series

Professor Robert Bor (Series Editor)
Chartered Psychologist and Registered Psychotherapist
Royal Free Hospital
London

Other titles in the Self-help Series:

Fly Away Fear
Elaine Iljon Foreman and Lucas Van Gerwen

COPING BETTER WITH CHRONIC FATIGUE SYNDROME/MYALGIC ENCEPHALOMYELITIS

Cognitive Behaviour Therapy for Chronic Fatigue Syndrome/Myalgic Encephalomyelitis (CFS/ME)

Bruce Fernie and Gabrielle Murphy

KARNAC

First published in 2009 by
Karnac Books Ltd
118 Finchley Road
London NW3 5HT

British Library Cataloguing in Publication Data

A C.I.P. for this book is available from the British Library

ISBN-13: 978-1-85575-537-6

Typeset by Vikatan Publishing Solutions (P) Ltd., Chennai, India

Printed in Great Britain

www.karnacbooks.com

CONTENTS

ACKNOWLEDGEMENTS   xi

ABOUT THE AUTHORS   xiii
- Dr Bruce Fernie   xiii
- Dr Gabrielle Murphy   xiii

FOREWORD   xv
- Coping Better with Chronic Fatigue Syndrome/
  Myalgic Encephalomyelitis (CFS/ME)   xv

INTRODUCTION   xvii
- How this book was written   xviii
- What is CBT?   xviii
- Depression and CFS/ME   xix
- What causes CFS/ME?   xx
- If we don't know the cause, how can we treat it?   xx
- About the design of this book   xx

CHAPTER ONE
Critical incidents, vulnerability factors
   and maintaining factors 1
- Critical incidents 2
- Vulnerability factors 3
- Maintaining factors 7

CHAPTER TWO
Goal setting 11
- Why set goals? 11
- SMART goals 12
- Energy-efficient goals 15
- The cycle of goal setting 18
- Planning to achieve your goal 18
- Baselines 19
- Managing baselines 20
- Making progress 20
- Bringing it all together 22
- Flexibility 22

CHAPTER THREE
Thoughts and feelings 23
- Negative automatic thoughts 24
- Alternative view 25
- Thoughts and feelings 25
- Thought and feelings diary 27
- Thought chains 28

CHAPTER FOUR
Sleep 31
- Why do we sleep? 31
- Microsleep 32
- How much sleep do we need? 32
- Sleep debt 33
- The stages of sleep 33

- Circadian rhythms   34
- Monitoring sleep and activity   34
- Sleep efficiency   36
- Factors that may contribute to poor quality sleep   37
- Problematic beliefs about sleep   39
- Strategies and techniques for improving sleep   40

CHAPTER FIVE
Activity   45
- Traffic lights   46
- Guide for interpreting your own activity diary   49
- Boom and bust   50

CHAPTER SIX
Energy capsules   53

CHAPTER SEVEN
Impact crosses   57

CHAPTER EIGHT
Challenging unhelpful patterns of thinking   65
- Mind the GAAAP   66
- Identifying thinking errors   67
- Your own use of thinking errors   70
- Alternative thoughts   71
- Taking the iTEST   71
- iTest   72
- Take your thought to court   73
- Tally the advantages and disadvantages   73

CHAPTER NINE
Stress and anxiety   79
- Fight or flight response   80
- Stress   81
- Worry   81

- Techniques for dealing with worry and stress   82
- Positive and negative beliefs about worry   83
- Stop signals   88
- Reframing a worry as a goal   88
- Example of reframing technique   89
- Acute anxiety or panic   90

CHAPTER TEN
Core beliefs   95
- Rules for living   97
- Vulnerability factors, rules for living and core beliefs   98
- Other ways to identify core beliefs   101
- Looking for themes in your unhelpful thoughts diary   101
- The 'what does that mean if that is true?' technique   102
- Modifying core beliefs   102
- New beliefs   107

CHAPTER ELEVEN
Symptom mapping   109
- Learning to listen and understand your body   109
- What are setbacks and relapses?   109
- Warning signs, recovery signs and natural responses   110
- What to do if you experience a warning sign
  symptom   113
- Symptom mapping   113

CHAPTER TWELVE
Planning for setbacks   117
- Distinguishing between a CFS/ME and
  a non-CFS/ME setback   118
- Possible contributing factors to a CFS/ME relapse   120
- Changes in patterns of sleep   120
- Changes in levels of activity   121
- Changes in emotional state   121
- New stressors   121

CHAPTER THIRTEEN
Medical perspective   123
- Fatigue as protective mechanism?   124
- Fatigue as a maladaptive mechanism?   124
- Joined up Government?   125
- Psycho-neuro-immunology   127
- Calling ME names?   129
- Explaining names   130
- Criteria   131
- Who gets CFS/ME?   133
- Is CFS/ME hereditary?   134
- To repeat the question, why CBT?   134
- Some practicalities   134

ACKNOWLEDGEMENTS

We would like to acknowledge the work of others and of our colleagues, both past and present, and their role in the design and content of this book. This book adapts ideas from the work of Mary Burgess, Trudie Chalder, Adrian Wells, Rona Moss-Morris, among others. Also, many of the interventions contained within were developed through working with our colleagues, Nathan Butler (Graded Exercise Therapist) and Karen Levy (Graded Activity Therapist) in the Fatigue Service at the Royal Free Hampstead NHS Trust.

We would also like to give special thanks to Marcantonio Spada, Annika Lindberg, Judith Smit, Kate Castle, Vincent Fannon, and Emma Milam for their help and support in writing this book.

ABOUT THE AUTHORS

Dr Bruce Fernie

Bruce is a chartered counselling psychologist at the Fatigue Service at the Royal Free Hampstead NHS Trust. He also works as a psychologist for CASCAID, an HIV mental health service within South London and Maudsley NHS Trust. He has worked in CFS/ME for four years in which he has coordinated the development of, and co-facilitated, the evidence-based group programmes designed to help those diagnosed with CFS/ME. As well as CFS/ME, his research interests lie in procrastination, metacognition and Self-Regulatory Executive Function theory.

Dr Gabrielle Murphy

Gabrielle is a physician working in the Fatigue Service at the Royal Free Hospital where she is the Clinical Lead. She also works in the Department of HIV medicine. Her interests include medically unexplained symptoms. Gabrielle is actively involved in local and national organisations promoting access to CFS/ME services and ongoing research.

FOREWORD

Coping Better with Chronic Fatigue Syndrome/Myalgic Encephalomyelitis (CFS/ME)

CFS/ME is a debilitating disorder which affects both physical and psychological functioning. It is also a poorly understood condition which was not widely accepted as a specific disorder until only a few years ago. Cognitive Behaviour Therapy (CBT), in conjunction with other physical and medical therapies, is now generally accepted as the treatment of choice for people who are affected by CFS/ME. The Fatigue Service at the Royal Free Hospital, London is highly regarded and is among the foremost clinical treatment centres worldwide for this condition. The Royal Free Hospital Fatigue Service provides the most up to date, evidence-based treatments, reflecting the NICE guidelines for clinical practice for this condition as well as the vast experience accumulated by the multi-disciplinary team. The symptoms of CFS/ME are diverse and sometimes confusing and difficult to discern. CFS/ME as a syndrome is complex clinically and can be a challenge to diagnose and treat. The authors of this self-help book recognise that patients cope better and are more likely to overcome their condition when they are partners in care. To this end, they encourage patients to become actively involved in monitoring their symptoms; challenging unhelpful thoughts; overcoming some of the physical and emotional challenges that they may encounter, and changing patterns in their behaviour. In order to enhance the effectiveness of their treatment, they engage patients in undertaking some of this work on their own between therapy and treatment sessions. This book provides the perfect companion for patients to develop and apply new insights into overcoming some of their specific symptoms as well as coping with the syndrome, both during the course of their therapy and afterwards. It provides a helpful structure and framework for understanding CFS/ME and its effects as well as practical exercises to help address some of the symptoms that patients may experience. By working systematically through the exercises in the book, readers can expect to gain further insight into their condition as well as confidence in managing and overcoming it. They can do so in the knowledge that the ideas come from a sought after clinical centre and are based on the most useful and modern approaches.

The book is thoroughly practical, free from abstract and difficult to understand psychological terms or 'psychobabble'. It conveys a positive message that patients suffering from CFS/ME can enjoy better physical and mental health. As the editor for this series of Karnac self-help books, it gives me great pleasure to introduce this highly practical and insightful new title. 'Coping Better with Chronic Fatigue Syndrome/Myalgic Encephalomyelitis' which is essential reading for anyone affected by the often poorly understood health problem, and for those who care for them.

Professor Robert Bor DPhil CPsychol CSci
FBPsS UKCP Reg FRAeS
Consultant Clinical Psychologist
in the Medical Specialities Directorate
Royal Free Hospital, London

INTRODUCTION

You have probably bought this book because either you have been given a diagnosis of Chronic Fatigue Syndrome/Myalgic Encephalomyelitis (CFS/ME) or you suspect that you may have this debilitating condition. Perhaps you have a friend or family member who suffers from CFS/ME and you want to better understand what is happening to them, and what may help them to cope better with their condition.

Chronic Fatigue Syndrome is a complex condition that has been given a variety of other names. The condition is also known as Myalgic Encephalomyelitis or ME, or you might know it as Chronic Fatigue Immunological Dysfunction Syndrome (CFIDS), or even Post Viral Fatigue Syndrome (PVFS). No matter what the label, the condition is characterised by extreme fatigue that does not improve with rest or sleep.

In this book, we will use the term Chronic Fatigue Syndrome/Myalgic Encephalomyelitis, abbreviated to CFS/ME. We recognise that these are not the labels preferred by everyone, and that both are contentious. We hope that this choice of label does not put you off working through the book and gaining benefit.

The diagnosis of CFS/ME is given when your doctor or doctors have been unable to attribute your symptoms to any other disease process. This in itself can be worrying—being told you have a medical condition that has had or is having a major impact on your life, yet no-one can point a finger at a cause. You may have heard horror stories about people being burdened by CFS/ME for many years, and this, quite naturally, has probably increased your anxiety and your stress level. On top of which, you may have encountered those who do not believe you are ill at all nor take your condition seriously. Some media reports may have condoned this view, by using dismissive terminology such as 'yuppie flu'.

Our intention with this book is to provide an explanation for CFS/ME by using an approach that incorporates a view that is both holistic and evidence-based.

How this book was written

In writing this book, we have tried to address concerns raised by the many patients we see at the Royal Free Hospital Fatigue Service about the strategies and tools we describe in this book. We have tried to pre-empt questions by addressing issues which are commonly raised by our patients.

Before we begin introducing the strategies and tools, we will first discuss some of the issues and concerns that are often mentioned in association with the use of Cognitive Behaviour Therapy (CBT) in the treatment of CFS/ME.

What is CBT?

CBT is a type of psychological therapy that looks at the interaction between thoughts, behaviour, emotions, physiology, and environment. Using a psychological therapy to treat CFS/ME does not mean that the condition is a psychological disorder.

Our position is that most, if not all, illnesses have a psychological aspect. When we are ill, our thoughts and behaviour determine how we respond to our symptoms, and different responses will have different effects on the illness.

Imagine that you have caught a cold—an illness with a clear biomedical cause (a virus). You think (cognition) to yourself that the best way of ridding yourself of this cold is to go for a 3-mile run (behaviour) in your shorts, in the rain. If this is the way you respond to your cold, it is likely that this kind of thinking and behaviour will prolong the duration of your cold. Clearly this is a ludicrous example that describes a pattern of thinking and behaviour that most people probably wouldn't engage in; however, it does illustrate our point that thinking and behaviour can impact on illnesses with a physical cause.

CBT has been shown to help people with a variety of problems, both psychological and physical. Reading this book does not guarantee a recovery, but we hope that the application of the strategies and tools will help you cope better with your CFS/ME.

Depression and CFS/ME

Depression and CFS/ME are separate disorders. While it is true that low levels of energy are symptoms of both depression and CFS/ME, this does not mean that they are the same illness. Equally, individuals with CFS/ME often experience low mood, frustration, and stress, but this also does not mean that such individuals are clinically depressed—these are often the emotional consequences of trying to live with a debilitating condition. Conversely people with CFS/ME can be clinically depressed, just as anybody else can. We believe it is important to make this distinction.

What causes CFS/ME?

At present we cannot say with any degree of certainty what causes CFS/ME. However, later in this book, we include a discussion of current biomedical theory. Regardless of the various theories of causation, we hope the strategies and tools described in this book may still be of benefit.

In our view it is unlikely that a single cause of CFS/ME will be found. We believe CFS/ME to be a complicated condition that most likely has causal and contributory factors that come from a variety of sources. This view is explained in more detail in the next chapter.

If we don't know the cause, how can we treat it?

We don't always need to know the cause of a disorder in order to treat it in a way that promotes better management and even recovery. For example, if somebody fractures a bone in their leg, a doctor does not necessarily need to know whether the fracture was caused by a football accident or by tripping on an uneven pavement slab. Either way, the likely treatment is for the leg to be immobilised in a plaster cast, and the likely outcome of this treatment is that the fracture will heal without complication.

About the design of this book

This book describes tools and techniques in a deliberate order. We recommend that you work through the book in the order it is presented and try all of the techniques described, even if initially you do not think that they will benefit you. It might be that it will take some time repeating and practicing the techniques described within before the full benefit is appreciated.

The first chapter provides a context for the rest of the book by outlining some of the factors that may make people more vulnerable to acquiring CFS/ME. Further discussion relates to the factors that may be helping to maintain or inhibit the management of CFS/ME.

CBT is not a passive therapy. It involves monitoring activity, sleep, thoughts and behaviour, trying out new strategies, and completing homework tasks. CBT is not a quick fix therapy, but we hope by patiently working through this book, you will learn strategies and tools that will help you to cope better with CFS/ME.

CHAPTER ONE

Critical incidents, vulnerability factors and maintaining factors

While we do not know precisely what causes CFS/ME, for many people there seems to be certain sets of 'critical incidents' that coincide with the onset of their CFS/ME, as well as certain 'vulnerability factors' that may have increased their chances of acquiring CFS/ME. Examining what these might be for you may seem a little like shutting the stable door once the horse has bolted, but we think that figuring out what these might be is an important part of your recovery, and may affect decisions you make in the future. Before we get on to that, we will explain what we mean by critical incidents.

A critical incident is an event or series of events that were happening in your life about the time you acquired CFS/ME. Some people might have been ill with some kind of viral infection; others might have experienced some kind of trauma or stress—like bereavement, divorce, or a loss of a job. Many people may have experienced a combination different factors. For some people, it might be difficult to identify a particular 'trigger' for their CFS/ME. Their CFS/ME may have gradually developed over a few years, as they experienced more and more of these stressful events.

1

A vulnerability factor refers to characteristics that may have helped to shape an individual's response to a critical incident. For example, a very driven individual who places great emphasis on achievement in a work or study setting may respond to being ill (critical incident) by continuing to work, believing that they should not take time off, because perhaps it conflicts with their work ethic, or they may perceive it as a sign of weakness. A vulnerability factor can be internal (e.g. being a highly motivated and driven individual), or external (e.g. pressure from work).

We will begin by looking at a few vignettes describing the initial experiences of individuals with CFS/ME. On reading, you might find that you can relate to aspects of these histories. Also, as you read, consider what might constitute a critical incident and a vulnerability factor for the individuals.

Example 1

> *Vincent has been suffering from CFS/ME for eight years. He used to be a self-employed carpenter and worked very hard to get his business off the ground. He was determined that he would build an excellent reputation for producing the highest quality work and beating deadlines. Vincent picked up a viral infection just about the same time as he heard that he had won a contract to work on a new housing development. The contract was very important to his business and so he worked through his illness, ignoring his symptoms. Eventually, he could no longer continue and he 'crashed' and took to bed. He experienced severe fatigue, tender lymph nodes, and joint ache. He spent the best part of the next three months in bed, and although he completed the contract for the housing development, he was unable to take on any new work and his business became impossible to sustain.*

Critical incidents

In Vincent's case, it would seem that his CFS/ME may have been triggered by a combination of a viral infection, working hard whilst he was ill, and perhaps the stress of fulfilling the obligations of the new contract for his business.

Vulnerability factors

Vincent seems to have set some very high standards for himself. There is a hint that Vincent might be a perfectionist—what with his drive to always produce the highest quality work and always finish before the deadline. It could be that this vulnerability factor led him to continue to work hard despite the fact that he was ill.

In Vincent's line of work, and especially when building up a business, it is very important to produce high quality work in order to develop a positive reputation. The consideration should perhaps have been to manage his health as a priority, as his business depended on his continued well-being.

Questions

What else could Vincent have done when he first became ill and had won the new contract for the housing development?

How *could* have he responded to these critical incidents?

Example 2

Anna is a 31 year old woman. About four years ago her mother became ill. Anna juggled her time between her husband, her job and looking after her mother. Two years ago, Anna's marriage ended in divorce. Although Anna and her husband did not have any children, the divorce was 'messy'. Around this time, Anna noticed that she was feeling more fatigued than usual. However, she did her best to continue caring for her mother. Her fatigue became worse and she began to develop other symptoms like tender lymph nodes and muscular aches and pains. She went to see a doctor, who told her that she was depressed and prescribed anti-depressants. Her mood and her fatigue improved a little, but she did not make a complete recovery. Currently, she is still fatigued and has developed a variety of other symptoms. She has had to give up work, but on good days she goes to see her mother and tries to help with the housework.

In the box below, write down what you think might have been the critical incident(s) in Anna's case. Also, try to think what the vulnerability factors were for Anna—write these down too. Ask yourself what aspects of Anna's character may have contributed to her taking on so much (e.g. trying to make her marriage work, keeping up with her career and taking on the care of her ill mother)? What was it about Anna that resulted in her not making other arrangements to care for her mother—even after Anna herself began to feel ill?

Potential critical incidents

How did she respond to these critical incidents?

Vulnerability factors

Now it is time to start applying these concepts of vulnerability factors and critical incidents to you. What was going on in your life about the time that you first became ill? Could any of these events be potential critical incidents? Our memories can be sketchy, so if you have a partner or close friend who knew you then, perhaps ask them to see if they can also recall what was going on in your life about the time you first became ill.

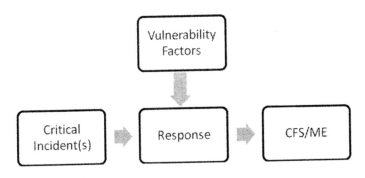

Once you have identified your own potential critical incidents, ask yourself how you responded to them. Does your response suggest anything about you? Does it suggest anything about the factors that may have made you more vulnerable to acquiring CFS/ME? In the first example above, Vincent's response to becoming ill with a viral infection and having a deadline to meet was to continue to work. You might think that one of his vulnerability factors was that he is a bit of a perfectionist, or that he placed great emphasis on his reputation, or that he was determined not to let other people down, or maybe something else altogether. When you are trying to think about vulnerability factors for yourself, try to generate as many ideas as possible. Try to let yourself 'think free'— don't filter out ideas that seem untrue at this point. Remember that the vulnerability factors that you have identified will have determined how you responded to your own critical incidents. If you find this difficult, perhaps start by noting how you responded to the critical incidents you have identified, then ask someone else whether they would have responded differently than you. If they would have responded differently, what does this difference say about you?

Please complete the exercise below by noting down the critical incidents you have identified and how you responded to them, as well as the vulnerability factors that you have been able to identify.

Possible critical incidents

How did you respond to these critical incidents?

Vulnerability factors

For the moment, we will leave these vulnerability factors, although we will be looking at them again in more depth in a later chapter. Instead, we shall move on a look at factors that might be (a) helping to maintain your CFS/ME, (b) acting as an obstacle to your recovery, and/or (c) increasing the severity of your symptoms. For simplicity's sake, we shall refer to all of these as maintaining factors.

Maintaining factors

There are numerous potential maintaining factors, some of which are illustrated in the diagram below. You may spot some factors that you think are missing, or some that you might believe don't apply to you. Feel free to amend the diagram as you see fit.

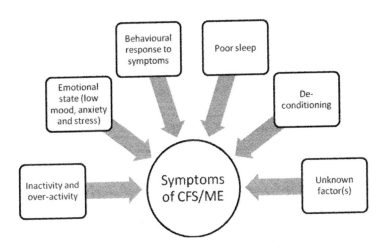

Much like the vulnerability factors, maintaining factors can also be internal and external. It might be useful for you to figure out whether the factors maintaining your CFS/ME are internal, or external, or a mixture of both. The tables below might help you to do this. Internal factors can often be influenced by changing our patterns of thinking (i.e. identifying unhelpful ways of thinking and learning new ways of thinking), and external factors can sometimes be addressed by changing our environment (often through changing our behaviour). It should be noted at this point that more often than not, changing our behaviour requires that we first change our thinking.

Let's look at how the different maintaining factors can contribute to CFS/ME symptoms.

Inactivity and over-activity

Often people with CFS/ME seem to follow a certain pattern of behaviour such that they are over-active when they are having a 'good day', and consequently this may lead to a 'flare-up' of symptoms, resulting in periods of imposed inactivity. This pattern of 'booming and busting' is reviewed in more detail in Chapter 5.

Internal	External
Feelings of frustration with the limitations imposed by CFS/ME. Beliefs about not wanting to let others down.	*Pressure from friends, family and work to engage in activities.*

Emotional state (low mood, anxiety, and stress)

Feelings of frustration and depression can be both mentally and physically exhausting. Indeed, fatigue and lethargy are common symptoms in depression. This is not to say that depression is the cause of your CFS/ME; if low mood is a problem for you however, it may contribute to your feelings of fatigue. Additionally, many people with CFS/ME report that when they are under stress, their symptoms are more intense.

Internal	External
Having unhelpful negative ways of thinking.	*Challenging life events: e.g. bereavements, job loss, and/or disability.*

Behavioural response to symptoms

People with CFS/ME may experience a bewildering array of symptoms. Some of the ways that people respond to these symptoms may be helpful, other ways may be less so.

Internal	External
Being unsure about how to interpret and respond to specific symptoms. This is made even more confusing as there seem to be different consequences for different symptoms for different people. For example, some people might find doing yoga leads to more muscle ache, whilst for others it does not.	*Pressure from society: e.g. adverts that tell us to take a few paracetamol and return to work as soon as possible after suffering from flu!*

Poor sleep

Lack of sleep or poor quality sleep can contribute to fatigue as well as poor concentration and irritability.

Internal	External
Irregular bed times.	*Background noise from neighbours, television or traffic.*
Poor sleep hygiene (discussed in chapter 4).	*Woken by children.*
Worrying while in bed.	*Working night shifts.*

De-conditioning

Long periods of little or no activity lead to body de-conditioning. This will further contribute to your feelings of fatigue and general sense of ill-being. Our bodies need constant maintenance to achieve a steady baseline of fitness.

Internal	External
Responding to some symptoms in such a way that further aggravates de-conditioning.	*Advice from others to take extended bed rest.*

Unknown factor(s)

By this we are primarily referring to biomedical factors that may both contribute to the cause and maintenance of CFS/ME. This is expanded on in chapter 13. There are many aspects to this complex condition that we cannot explain.

CHAPTER TWO

Goal setting

So far we have discussed vulnerability factors, critical incidents and maintaining factors, and we hope that you are now familiar with these terms. One of the primary goals of this book is to provide you with strategies and tools to help you address the maintaining factors that you have identified. But, before we start this, it is useful to establish some personal goals. At the moment, if this is the first time you have read through this book, you may not have all of the strategies and tools you need to achieve the goals that you set yourself. However, we believe that it is important to set some goals first, because they may provide a context for the strategies and tools you learn in later chapters. We hope that by setting goals first, you will see that the techniques described in this book have an immediate practical application.

Why set goals?

Energy is a precious commodity for people with CFS/ME. The setting of well-defined goals is important because it allows us to allocate our energy efficiently. If we don't know exactly what we want to achieve, we may end up aimlessly wasting our energy on activities and tasks that do not result in sufficient 'payback'. Reaching goals gives us a sense of achievement, and may help to alleviate some of the frustration experienced with CFS/ME.

SMART goals

Perhaps in your current state it is difficult to think of a goal, or perhaps the only goal you can think of is to get better. While 'getting better' may seem like a great goal to have, it is vague.

Specific	SMART goals are specific goals. Rather than making your goal something vague like 'to go out more', try and make it something specific like 'to go to my local café to meet a friend for a nice cup of tea once a week for an hour'.
Measurable	If a goal is measurable, not only is it easier to figure out when you have achieved it, you can also work out how close you are to achieving it.
Achievable	A goal is achievable if it is possible. There will be things you can do right now, and other things that you cannot. However, there will be some things that you might not be able to do now, but could be achievable for you in the future.
Relevant	Is the goal something that is relevant to you? One way of assessing how relevant a goal is for you, is to see if it is 'energy efficient'—we will discuss this idea in more detail later in this chapter.
Timed	It is useful to set yourself some kind of time limit for your goal, but it is also important to ensure that your time limit is realistic.

Vague goals are difficult to plan for because we don't have a clear way of telling what it is that we are trying to work towards. For example, what does 'getting better' actually mean? Does it mean 'better than you are now', if so, how much better? Does it mean doing more things than you are doing now, or does it mean doing the same amount of things you are doing now, but for these activities to be less painful and less draining? Does it mean living life exactly as you did before you became ill? Some of you may have been ill for a long time, and as much as we would like to have the energy of a 20 year old, this gets more and more difficult to achieve as the years roll by. Besides, after reading Chapter 1, you may decide that actually things weren't so great before you acquired CFS/ME anyway. You might have identified certain aspects of how you were living your life that may have made you more vulnerable to CFS/ME.

When you set your goal, try not to become too concerned with your current limitations. Think about making your goal something you cannot achieve now, but would like to be able to achieve later. Remember, part of making a goal achievable is giving yourself enough time to accomplish your goal.

Below we have an example SMART goal sheet and provide a blank SMART goal sheet for you to complete. We suggest that you try to generate as many SMART goals as possible, in which case you will most likely need a few more blank sheets of paper.

Example SMART goal

SMART Goal	Date to Achieve Goal
To go for an evening meal at a restaurant with a friend once a fortnight	6 months from today

Continued on next page

Is this goal SMART?	
Specific	*Yes*
Measurable	*Yes*
Achievable	*Yes*
Relevant	*Yes*
Timed	*Yes*

Blank SMART goal sheets

SMART goal	Date to achieve goal

Is this goal SMART?
Specific
Measurable
Achievable
Relevant
Timed

SMART goal	Date to achieve goal

Is this goal SMART?
Specific
Measurable
Achievable
Relevant
Timed

Energy-efficient goals

Many people with CFS/ME find that energy is in short supply. This makes it extra important to ensure that your goals are energy-efficient. What we mean by this is to make sure that you are getting as big a payoff as possible for the energy that you are investing in your goal. One way of helping you to assess the size of the payoff for achieving a goal is to estimate how many areas of your life that the goal would benefit.

In order to work out the potential payoff of a goal, it might be helpful to step back and consider all the factors that make up your life. Once you have done this, it is useful to consider whether the SMART goals that you have chosen would impact on the different aspects of your life.

For example, you might choose to divide your life up into the following pieces:

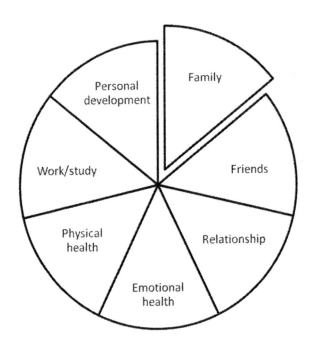

Of course, it is up to you how you choose to divide your life. However, don't dismiss pieces just because they are not part of your life at the moment. For example, you may not be in a relationship at the moment, but this does not necessarily mean relationships are never going to be part of your life. It might be worth considering including 'relationships' because it is possible that one of your goals could affect this area. Your goal might make it more likely that you could meet somebody with whom you could have a relationship, or perhaps you might be in a relationship by the time you get to achieve your goal.

Take a moment to specify all the pieces that make up your life, or may describe it in the future. You can use the table below as a template. Once you have divided up your life in this way, ask yourself whether achieving your SMART goal would benefit each component in turn. This, like most things in life, is not an exact science. Try to reason it through. Perhaps you could ask a close friend or family member for help. We recommend doing this exercise on a piece of paper, rather than in your head. Putting down these thoughts on paper can help to clarify things and reduce confusion.

SMART goal		
To go for an evening meal at a restaurant with a friend once a fortnight		
Life piece	Does my SMART goal impact on this area of my life, if so how?	
Family	*Yes*	*This could be an area of my life that benefits from achieving my goal. If I am able to go to a restaurant with a friend, I might also be able to go out with a family member. Also, getting out of the house might actually be beneficial for some of the members of my family!*

Continued on next page

SMART Goal

Friends	Yes	*This would clearly be an area of my life improved by achieving my goal. Over the last few years, I have been spending less and less time with my friends—going out with them for a meal might be a good way of reinforcing my friendships.*
Relationship	Yes	*This might be an area that benefits from achieving my goal. If I am able to cope with a restaurant with a friend, I might also be able to cope with dinner dates as my confidence grows.*
Emotional health	Yes	*I have not been able to cope with restaurants for years. Indeed, I have not done very much at all that I would consider fun over the last few years. If I can achieve my goal, I think it make me feel pretty good.*
Physical health	Yes	*In order to achieve my goal, I will have had to improve my stamina. I would be doing more than I am doing now, and this would mean that I had improved my physical health.*
Work/study	Maybe	*This would be indirectly benefited by achieving my goal. I guess if I am able to engage in conversation, go out in public, handle the travel, and sit up for a couple of hours, it would mean that I might be better able to cope with work/study.*
Personal development	Yes	*If I achieve this goal, I would be doing something I have not done for years. It would be a sign that I am improving, and therefore, for me it would represent personal growth.*

So, the example SMART goal (*'to go for an evening meal at a restaurant with a friend once a fortnight'*) scores six and a half out of the seven life components. This goal would seem to have the potential of making a beneficial impact in lots of different areas, and therefore it would seem to be an energy-efficient goal and worth pursuing.

The cycle of goal setting

Goal setting is a cyclical process. First, you set yourself some SMART goals, and then you test to see if the goals that you have chosen are 'energy-efficient': i.e. a good use of your precious energy. If it is not, then go back and try to generate some alternative SMART goals and test these to see if they have the potential for a greater payoff.

Planning to achieve your goal

Now that you have chosen a goal that is both SMART and energy-efficient it is time to make a plan to help you achieve it. There are two main steps in this process: the first is to deconstruct the goal (i.e. work out what are the component parts that make up the goal), and second, to plot a graded step-by-step plan that can lead you gently to achieving your goal. We shall use the example goal above to illustrate this process, and then you can try it for yourself.

In the example above, we have broken down the overall goal (*'to go for an evening meal at a restaurant with a friend once a fortnight'*) into four component parts, or sub-goals. This goal seems to involve (1) going out in public, (2) sitting up for two hours, (3) engaging in conversation for two hours, and (4) journeying to and from the restaurant.

It is best to deal with each component separately. Now we need to break down each of the sub-goals into small manageable steps. The first step should be something that you can manage

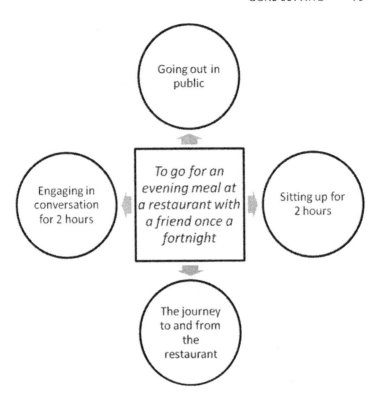

Going out in
public

Engaging in
conversation
for 2 hours

To go for an
evening meal at
a restaurant with
a friend once a
fortnight

Sitting up for
2 hours

The journey
to and from
the
restaurant

Step 1: Deconstructing your goal.

now, in your current state. We will use the 'engaging in conversation for two hours' sub-goal to illustrate what we mean.

Baselines

So now you need to work out how long you can engage in conversation without making your symptoms worse. This would be your 'conversation baseline'. How you feel probably varies from day-to-day, but your conversation baseline should remain constant. The important thing to focus on when you are working out your baseline for any activity is whether your symptoms change over the course of engaging it. For example, you might begin your conversation already feeling bad, but as long as you don't feel any worse by the end of it, you would not have exceeded your baseline.

Managing baselines

With some activities, like walking or reading, keeping within your baseline is relatively simple. For example, if your 'reading baseline' is 15 minutes, you can simply put your book down when the time has expired. If your 'walking baseline' is 10 minutes, you could walk in one direction for 5 minutes and then turn back. However, not all activity baselines will be so straightforward to manage. Addressing this problem will require some imaginative thinking.

Let's take the 'conversation baseline' as an example. The question is how do you break down or deconstruct the process of engaging in conversation into smaller steps? Putting boundaries on over day activities like these can be difficult. However, there are several ways you could address this problem. We suggest making these options as natural as possible. Conversations on the telephone might be easier to time-manage than face-to-face conversations. Perhaps it is more natural and easier to say, 'I am sorry but I have to go now' and end a conversation on the telephone than it would be to say this to someone's face? Maybe visiting friends (if this is feasible for you) rather than friends visiting you gives you more control over the duration of your conversation, because you can decide when you want to leave. None of these solutions are perfect, but making progress is not about being perfect: instead, it is about being good enough.

Making progress

Once you have worked out your baseline for an activity, practice repeating the activity over several days without exceeding

Step 1: conversation
for 10 minutes

Step 2: conversation
for 15 minutes

Step 3: conversation
for 25 minutes

Step n: conversation
for 2 hours

your baseline. Once you have done this and established your baseline, introduce a small increase to your baseline. You then practice your new baseline until you became used to it. If you are finding your new baseline too challenging, it could be because the increment was too great. Review your baseline until you find a level at which you are comfortable without making your symptoms worse.

Bringing it all together

Once you have achieved all of the sub-goals, it is time to bring all of the components that you have practiced together. Remember that because you might be bringing together several components at the same time, this might be a little overwhelming. It may be a good idea to break down the overall goal into steps, just as you have done with the sub-goals.

Flexibility

It is important to remain flexible both with the goals that you set for yourself and how you have planned to achieve them. Hopefully, as you read through the rest of this book, you will learn new strategies and tools that you may decide to use to help you achieve your goals. Indeed, as you read through the rest of this book, you may find that you want to change the goals that you have come up with.

Thoughts and feelings

One of the central ideas behind CBT is that there is a relationship between our thoughts and our emotional state. In later chapters, we will expand on this to include the relationship between our thoughts, emotional state, physiology and behaviour.

The idea is that it is not situations themselves that upset us, but instead it is how we interpret them. There tends to be more than one way of interpreting any situation, and the interpretation that we make has consequences for our emotional state.

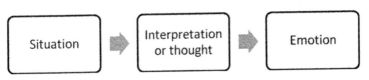

It may seem that other ways of interpreting a situation are less true or even not true at all; this does not mean however that there are no alternative potential interpretations of a situation. We will look at why people might have a tendency to interpret a situation in a *particular way* in a later chapter. For now, we will try to illustrate the relationship between our thinking and our emotions.

Situation

Helen is walking down a busy high street and sees one of her friends walking toward her. Helen smiles and says hello, but her friend does not acknowledge her and walks straight past.

Cognition (thought)

Helen thinks to herself that she must have done something to upset her friend, and that her friend no longer likes her.

Emotion

Helen feels sad and miserable, and even angry. And so stays at home instead of going out for the evening.

Consequences

Because she stays at home, she misses out on what could have been a fun evening. Instead, she ruminates (dwells) on what happened earlier. She remembers all the other times when she has felt overlooked, and concludes that she has few friends. This makes her feel sad, worthless and hopeless.

Negative automatic thoughts

Sometimes the thoughts that we have occur so quickly we are almost not consciously aware of them: these are known as 'automatic thoughts'. Thoughts become automatic through

Alternative view

Of course it could be true—her friend may no longer like her—however, in that situation, Helen did not have enough information to be sure about that judgement. It did not occur to her that her friend could simply have not noticed her—it was a busy high street and her friend was day-dreaming and not paying attention to anyone else.

repetition. If you drive, think back to when you were having driving lessons. Remember the first few times you were trying to change gear: you were most likely having lots of thoughts going through your head—the revs, your speed, where the next gear was on the stick, when to depress the clutch, etc. When you change gear now, you probably are less aware of all these thoughts. However, the thoughts need to be there somewhere in order to change gear successfully. It is just that your thoughts about changing gear have become automatic through repetition—from changing gear hundreds and thousands of times.

With practice we can learn to identify automatic thoughts. Usually a good clue is when our mood changes. If you notice this, try treating your thoughts like they were being played out on a video tape—press pause and then rewind to identify the automatic thought.

So at this stage we are going to use an emotion as a clue to identify any unhelpful thoughts that you might be having.

Thoughts and feelings

Thoughts often determine how we feel, and more often than not, there is more than one way of interpreting any situation. It is important therefore, to figure out exactly how and what we are thinking and to understand the influence this has on our mood and behaviour.

When you notice that you are feeling low, try to trace back to what you were thinking about just before your mood changed. Using the thought and feelings diary (next page), write down the situation that you were in when your mood changed, and then note down the thought (or thoughts) that you have identified. Once you have written down the thought(s), rate how strongly you believe them out of 100%, and then note how you are feeling (also rate the strength of your emotion out of 100%).

Date	Situation	Thought (rate strength of belief in thought out of 100%)	Feeling (rate intensity of feeling out of 100%)
25/9/08	Emma calls to invite me to meet for a coffee, but I am feeling very tired and I have to turn her down.	I am going to lose all my friends because of this illness (70%).	Sad (80%)
		I am never going to get better (65%).	Hopeless (90%)
		I can't even do the simplest of things like going for a coffee (90%).	Frustrated (80%)

It is important that you complete the thought and feelings diary as close as is possible to the low point in your mood. This will make it easier to identify the accompanying thought(s).

Thought and feelings diary

Date	Situation	Thought (rate strength of belief in thought out of 100%)	Feeling (rate intensity of feeling out of 100%)

Some people find it difficult to identify their automatic thoughts, others find it relatively easy. With perseverance and practice it becomes easier. This is a technique that is necessary for many of the strategies and tools that we will look at as you progress through the book. We recommend that, as you work through the chapters, you continue to complete the thoughts and feelings diary.

Thought chains

Sometimes you may note that your mood has changed and be able to identify what you were thinking about, but it may not seem immediately apparent that the thought you have identified is particularly unhelpful or negative. Often we need to delve a little deeper to work out the meanings that underlie our thoughts.

For example, imagine that you are thinking about speaking to your boss about taking rest periods throughout the day in order for you to help manage your CFS/ME. Imagine that the very thought of doing this results in you feeling quite anxious and stressed. It is important to try to find out what it is exactly about speaking to your boss regarding this issue that makes you feel anxious. One way of trying to identify these unhelpful thoughts is to use 'thought chains'. These 'thought chains' work by putting your first thought at the top of the chain, then asking yourself one of a few questions about the thought, putting your answer(s) in the next link in the chain. The idea is that you repeat this until you identify some underlying negative thoughts. There is an example below that might help you understand this process.

In the example below, two questions were used to forge the thought chains ('*What is the worst that could happen?*' and '*What would it mean if this happens?*'). However, these questions may not be relevant to your original thought. You may want to try '*What would this mean about me?*' or make up your own question if you can think of something more appropriate.

I have to speak to my boss and ask for some time off work

What is the worst that could happen?

Boss might say 'no'

What would it mean if this happens?

My boss might not believe that I am ill, and think that I am just lazy.

What would it mean if this happens?

My boss might fire me

The example generated a few potential unhelpful thoughts: e.g. 'Boss might say 'no', 'My boss might not believe that I am ill, and just think that I am lazy', and 'My boss might fire me'. Note that all of these thoughts are hypotheses: i.e. potentially they could be either true or false. At present, we would recommend that you practice identifying unhelpful thoughts using the techniques we have discussed. As we all know, it helps to know what the problem is before you attempt to solve it.

CHAPTER FOUR

Sleep

People with CFS/ME frequently report poor, or disturbed, sleep. People may sleep too much or too little, have non-refreshing sleep, and wake-up during the night. A disturbed sleep pattern can make it difficult to think clearly, make you feel irritable, make it difficult to concentrate and affect your memory, as well as increasing your fatigue.

Clearly, poor quality sleep does not explain all of the symptoms of CFS/ME; however, it is likely that, for some, it can contribute to some of the fatigue and deterioration in cognitive functions, like memory and concentration.

Why do we sleep?

Nobody knows for sure why we sleep; however, broadly speaking, there are two main hypotheses that attempt to answer this question. One idea is that sleep is a behaviour that has evolved because it served a purpose for our ancestors. It has been proposed that back when there were no sources of artificial light, it would have benefited our ancestors to seek out safe places to be immobile (as we are mostly when we sleep). Otherwise, running around in the dark would make us vulnerable to injury (falling down holes and the like) and to attack by predators whose night vision is superior to ours.

Another theory is that sleep performs a restorative function in that it enables the repair of day-to-day psychological and physical wear and tear. Either way, the need to sleep is one of the most powerful urges we experience.

Microsleep

If we are not getting enough sleep, we often experience an increase in the urge to sleep. In addition to this, we are also more likely to enter into what is known as microsleep. Microsleep lasts for about 5–10 seconds and describes a state where we might shut our eyes whilst being unresponsive to stimuli (e.g. sounds). Microsleep can impair our ability to concentrate on tasks that require us to focus our attention for long periods of time (e.g. reading a newspaper or book, watching a film, etc). This is because we are slipping into microsleep when we are attempting such tasks. This may also mean that our memory of whatever it was we were doing is also impaired, as we are not fully attending to the task as we were dropping in and out of microsleep. In sleep experiments where people are hooked up to various machines that monitor brain waves, the participants are often unaware that they have momentarily drifted off into microsleep, despite the experimenter's equipment indicating the contrary.

How much sleep do we need?

There is not a satisfactory answer to this question: the amount of sleep needed varies from individual to individual. Some individuals 'get by' with as little as 5 or 6 hours a night. In some extreme cases, individuals have been reported as functioning normally on as little as 1 hour a night! Others feel that they need as much as 10 hours per night.

Sleep debt

Sleep debt refers to the idea that if we miss out on say 4 hours of sleep one night, we need to balance our 'sleep books' by getting an extra 4 the next night. Research suggests that this idea is false. Indeed, in sleep deprivation experiments where individuals have not slept for over one hundred hours, when they are allowed to sleep for as long as they like after these extended sleep periods, they only 'make up' a few extra hours sleep for the first few nights and report no ill effects.

The stages of sleep

There are five stages of sleep. We pass up and down through these stages approximately every 90 minutes throughout the course of a night's sleep.

Stage 1:	This point is the crossover between wakefulness and sleep. It is a drowsy state and during this stage the eyelids will often open and close, and the eyes roll back.
Stage 2:	During this stage of sleep breathing and heart rate decreases, and muscles relax. People are sound asleep by this stage. However, sometimes if awoken at this point, people claim not to have been asleep at all.
Stage 3 & 4:	There are differences between stage 3 and 4 sleep, but these are not important to go into now. These stages describe when we are in a deep sleep. If we are woken from this state, we would probably feel quite confused and mumble incoherently.

Stage 5:   Stage 5 sleep is also known as Rapid Eye Movement (REM) sleep. This is the stage of sleep in which we dream and, as the name suggests, our eyes can be seen to move around under our eyelids. During this stage of sleep, many of our physiological responses, such as breathing and heart rate, are at waking levels. Some people report that they do not dream. This is not true, as we all dream 4 or 5 times a night. It is more the case that people cannot recall their dreams, rather than not dreaming at all. Sleep experiments show that if you wake people during their REM sleep, they are able to describe their dreams in vivid detail. During this stage of sleep, people tend not to be awoken by indiscriminate noises and sounds; however they are aroused by meaningful stimuli such as the calling of their name.

Circadian rhythms

Circadian rhythms describe our daily body clock. This lets our bodies know when it is time to sleep and when it is time to be active. Our body clock is reset by daylight. If left to run free, e.g. in environment of continuous light, our circadian rhythm would cycle every 25 hours, despite our days lasting for 24.

Monitoring sleep and activity

It is important that you find out exactly what is happening with your sleep. The easiest way to do this is by keeping a sleep diary like the one set out below. Continuing to monitor your sleep as you work through this book will help you to identify which techniques are having the most beneficial impact on you.

Example

	Mon	Tues	Wed	Thurs	Fri	Sat	Sun
Going to bed time	10 PM	7 PM	12 AM	11 PM	12 AM	2 AM	8 PM
Fell asleep at	12 AM	2 AM	3 AM	11.15 PM	12.45 AM	3 AM	11 PM
Woke up at	7 AM	11 AM	8 AM	9 AM	9.45 AM	12 PM	10 AM
Out of bed at	8 AM	2 PM	10 AM	10 AM	11.30 AM	2 PM	10:10 AM
Number of hours slept at night	7	9	5	9.45	9	9	11
Number of hours in bed	12	19	10	11	11.30	12	14.10
Number of naps during the day	2	1	4	1	0	0	0
Average length of naps	30 minutes	45 minutes	30 minutes	1 hour	–	–	–

Now complete your own sleep diary. There is an example blank diary below. It is best for you to complete it as you go through the next week, rather than try to remember what happened for the week just gone. We will use your sleep diary to try and work out what may be affecting your sleep. You may find it difficult to accurately record when you were able to fall asleep. However, just do your best. Even a rough estimate is better than nothing at all.

	Mon	Tues	Wed	Thurs	Fri	Sat	Sun
Going to bed time							
Fell asleep at							
Woke up at							
Out of bed at							
Number of hours slept at night							
Number of hours in bed							
Number of naps during the day							
Average length of naps							

Sleep efficiency

Sleep efficiency describes the relationship between how long we are in bed and how long we are actually asleep. Our sleep can be considered more efficient if the duration of our sleep is similar to the length of time we spend in bed. We can represent sleep efficiency by the simple equation shown below.

$$\frac{Duration\ of\ sleep}{Length\ of\ time\ in\ bed} = sleep\ efficiency$$

The closer the result of the equation is to 1, the more efficient your sleep.

$$\frac{7\ hours}{8\ hours} = 0.875$$

Now that you have completed your own sleep diary, you should be able to calculate your own sleep efficiency. Does your sleep efficiency vary greatly over the week? Is it close to 1?

Factors that may contribute to poor quality sleep

Look through the following factors, and with the help of your sleep diary, try to see if any of them might be affecting your sleep. If there is someone you trust who knows you well, perhaps try to recruit them to help you with this. Make a note of which of these factors affects you.

Irregular sleep pattern:	Going to sleep at differing times and napping during the day will disrupt your natural body (circadian) rhythm. This is because your body is not getting its light and activity cues to reset your circadian rhythm. This may result in you having trouble getting to sleep, having non-refreshing sleep and feeling tired during the day (leading to daytime napping).
Napping:	Daytime napping can be almost irresistible when we have a strong urge to sleep. However, studies show that if we nap in the day and have stage 3 & 4 sleep, we have less of this deep sleep during the night. This might explain why daytime napping leads to non-refreshing night-time sleep.

Poor sleep efficiency:	After calculating your sleep efficiency scores, you may have noted that you are spending a considerable amount of time in bed but not asleep. This will weaken the association that you have between bed and sleep, making it more difficult to sleep in future.
Daytime inactivity:	Daytime activities (e.g. working, cleaning, going for walks, reading, studying, etc) can act as cues to set your circadian rhythm. They work by teaching your body that it should be awake when you are doing them, and asleep when you are not.
Alcohol and stimulants:	Few people with CFS/ME report drinking too much alcohol, however drinking alcohol before bed, or having a coffee or tea (or any other drinks with caffeine), or even having a cigarette (because of the nicotine) will make it more difficult to fall asleep. It is best to not drink tea or coffee for at least four hours before you go to bed.
Worries:	It is strange that, for many of us, we engage in our most intense worrying when we are in bed. Worrying can make it more difficult to get to sleep.
Diet:	If you eat or drink too much before bed, both the process of digestion and the discomfort of food in your stomach as you lie in bed may interfere with sleep.
Exercise:	Exercising within three hours of bed will make it more difficult for you to wind down before you try to sleep.
Environment:	If you bedroom is too hot or too cold then it will be difficult to sleep. Also, if your mattress is uncomfortable or there is much noise, this will also interfere with trying to get to sleep. Ideally, your bedroom should be used for sleep alone and should not double up as a TV room and/or a study.

Problematic beliefs about sleep

We feel that it is important to look at some commonly held unhelpful beliefs about sleep. It seems that these beliefs often lead people to worry about their sleep, therefore making it more difficult to achieve quality sleep. The chances are that if you are trying hard to sleep, sleep is the last thing that you will be able to do.

- *I must get 8–10 hours sleep a night*
- *If I don't sleep something catastrophic will happen*
- *I'll get sick if I don't sleep*
- *If I do not get my 8 hours, I cannot function*
- *If I wake-up during the night then I am having a poor night's sleep*

We hope that you will already be questioning most of these myths about sleep having read through the beginning of this chapter. You will have read that there is no set minimum amount of sleep that human's need.

Research into how much sleep is essential and how we are affected by poor quality sleep shows that human beings are very resilient and some of us may function on minimal amounts without catastrophic consequences. It is also clear however that the ideal amount of sleep needed varies from person to person and is, of course, affected by the quality of that sleep that we have as well.

It also worth noting in respect to the final problematic belief about sleep listed above that it is very common for us to wake multiple times during the night. Mostly when this happens, we just roll over and go back to sleep, forgetting that we woke up by the time morning comes. Other times, of course, we wake because we need to use the bathroom. In such cases, it is best not just to roll over. However, if we wake during the night and think to ourselves that this is in some way a bad thing, we are more likely to start worrying, we will become mentally stimulated, and we will find it more difficult to get back to sleep.

Strategies and techniques for improving sleep

Now that you have identified some factors that may be impacting on the quality of your sleep, look through the list of strategies below to see if any of them may help. The list is by no means exhaustive, but hopefully you will be thinking of your own ways to address the factors that affect your sleep pattern.

Regulating or increasing activity during the day

If you engage in the same activities at the same time each day, this can help 'reprogram' your circadian rhythms (body clock), which in turn may influence your sleep pattern. You may also consider increasing the amount of activities you engage in during the day; however, we would recommend waiting until you have worked through chapter 5 before you consider any increase in activity.

Regulating the times that you go to bed and get up

This will help to set your body clock, it will help you fall asleep and improve the quality of your sleep. Initially, such regulation may be very difficult to achieve. Setting an alarm clock so that you get up at the same time every day may be a useful place to start. Eventually, this will make it easier to go to sleep at the same time in the night. Some people try jumping straight in to keeping a regular bedtime and waking-up time, other people prefer a more gentle approach: e.g. adjusting the time that they go to bed and wake-up every few days in 15 minute intervals.

Cutting out daytime napping

Again, some people cut out these naps straight away, others may find this too difficult. If it is too difficult, try reducing the length of your naps by 15 minutes every four or five days. You may find using an alarm clock makes this easier to do. It might be helpful to choose an alarm sound that is pleasant, rather than abrasive.

Associate bed with sleep

Your bed should be for sleep, and not for reading, watching TV, eating, drinking or worrying. If you have found that your sleep efficiency is poor (i.e. you are spending a lot of time in bed without sleeping), then get out of bed when you are not sleeping. If you have been lying in bed, trying to sleep for more than 20 minutes, then get out of bed, go to a different room, and do something that is not too stimulating (i.e. definitely do not have a cigarette or a cup of tea or coffee).

Improve bedroom environment

Try to ensure that your bedroom is not too hot or too cold. Ensure that you have a comfortable mattress and pillow. If your bedroom is noisy, consider trying out earplugs to stifle some of the excess noise.

Improve sleep hygiene

Do not eat large meals before bed.
Do not exercise within three hours of bed.
Do not drink tea, coffee, or any other caffeinated drink, or alcohol within four hours of your intended bedtime.

Worry period/book

Set aside half an hour a day in which you will deal with your worries, if you find yourself worrying outside of this period, note in a worry book what you are worrying about and say to yourself 'I am going to postpone my worries until my worry period'.

You may find that you are lying in bed worrying when you want to be falling asleep. If this is the case, get out of bed, go to a different room, and make a note of all of the worrying thoughts that are going through your mind in your worry book. This will make sure you do not forget your worry, and this may make it easier to postpone your worry until your worry period.

We will deal with worry in more detail in a later Chapter.

Wind down routine

Plan a wind down routine to begin an hour and a half before bed. This may include having a hot milky drink for some, stopping work, relaxing and taking a hot bath. If you can devise a routine that suits you and to which it is easy to adhere, eventually it may act as a cue to tell your brain it is ready to sleep.

You may find it helpful to make writing down your worries in your worry book part of your wind down routine. You may find that having recorded your worries before you go to bed means that it is less likely that you worry when you are in bed.

Pick some of the above strategies for you to implement over the next few weeks (and after). Try to choose strategies that address the factors that you have identified as affecting your sleep.

Sleep strategies to implement

_____

_____

_____

Try to implement these strategies one at a time. This will give you a better idea of which ones are benefiting you and which ones are not. Bear in mind that, if you have had sleep difficulties for some time, it will take a while for you to feel the benefit of these strategies.

It may be useful to plan a wind-down routine as well. This will make it easier to stick to. The more regular you can make it, the greater the chance that your brain will begin to recognise the routine as a cue for sleep.

Example wind-down routine

Record worries in worry book

Read

Wash and clean teeth

Relaxation/Meditation

Switch off lights

Go to bed

Wind-down routine

CHAPTER FIVE

Activity

Activity encompasses all that you do, day and night: it can be washing yourself, vacuum cleaning your carpets, going to work and even resting and sleeping. Some activities are physical, such as walking or shopping, others might be considered to be more 'cerebral', like using a computer or talking on the phone.

You may find that you do a lot less activity now than before you acquired CFS/ME, or you may find that you do too much activity for how you are feeling. In order to manage your symptoms, it best to get as much balance in your activity as possible. Sometimes this will be impossible because there will unanticipated events and demands. However, the more balance you can get into your life, the better.

The first step in trying to obtain balance in your life is to figure out what you are doing day-to-day. As we have said before, memory in CFS/ME can be sketchy, so it is a good idea to keep an activity diary. In addition to being an aide memoire, this will give you a much clearer picture of what you are doing with your week.

An activity diary is simply a weekly diary, in which you record all that you do. There is an example activity diary on the next page and a blank diary for you to use on the page after that. These diaries divide each day of the week into two hour blocks. If you wish, you own activity diary can be divided into one hour blocks. This is entirely up to you.

You might find it a little tiresome completing weekly diaries, but we recommend completing them for the moment anyway. Try to complete one that represents the closest you can get to an average week, for example not a week when you are on holiday or going to Buckingham Palace to get your MBE. If you really don't want to complete them every week, maybe use them every 2 or 4 weeks. Think of them as snapshots of your life at the moment. They can be a useful way of assessing whether the changes you implement based on the strategies and tools described in this book are having a beneficial effect on your life.

Traffic lights

After you have completed an activity diary, dig out some high-lighter pens or coloured pencils. Looking at you activity diary and using the colour key below, highlight each activity that you have engaged in during the last week according to how much energy it would demand. Don't worry if you don't have green, orange and red pens or pencils, as long as you have three different colours, you can use you own colour key.

Choosing an energy rating can be quite complex: the same activity might drain more of your energy on different days of the week or even times of the day. An activity might be more draining now you have CFS/ME than before you were ill.

A possible solution to this is to try to imagine that you were having a good day, and that you had no worries or stresses, and ask yourself how much energy would the activity demand in that scenario?

By taking this approach, we are aiming to establish the range and pattern of activity over a typical week for you and also how you felt during and after the various activities. How

Days	Monday	Tuesday	Wednesday	Thursday	Friday	Saturday	Sunday
8–10h00	Slept till 9, then made breakfast	Asleep	Ate breakfast, went to work	Asleep	Ate breakfast and went to work	Asleep	Asleep
10–12h00	Watched TV	Woke at 10h30	At work	Asleep	At work but had to leave as too fatigued	Get ready to go out for coffee	Local pool for a gentle swim
12–14h00	Watched TV	Went shopping	Break at work for one hour	Asleep	Nap	Coffee with Arlene	Family lunch
14–16h00	Ate Lunch	Shopping	At work	Lunch in front of TV	Nap	Nap	Nap
16–18h00	Napped for 30 minutes	Home: putting shopping away	Nap	Nap	Shopping	Housework	Read the newspapers
18–20h00	Spoke on telephone	Nap	Nap	listened to news on radio	Put shopping away	Nap	Lie down and listen to radio
20–22h00	Watched TV	Nap	Supper in front of TV	Made family phone calls	Made supper	Make Supper and watch TV	Supper
22–24h00	Watched TV	Watched TV	Watched TV	Bath and TV	Asleep	Asleep	TV
24h–08h00	Went to bed at midnight	Watched TV until 2AM	Watched TV until 01h00	Bed and asleep at 02h00	Asleep	Asleep	TV and sleep at 02h00

Days	Monday	Tuesday	Wednesday	Thursday	Friday	Saturday	Sunday
8–10h00							
10–12h00							
12–14h00							
14–16h00							
16–18h00							
18–20h00							
20–22h00							
22–24h00							
24h–08h00							

you felt whilst you were doing them is likely to depend on lots of different factors. So it might be worth attempting to unpick the complex factors that are (a) maintaining your CFS/ME, (b) acting as an obstacle to your recovery, and/or (c) intensifying your symptoms by focussing in on behaviours.

Note that high energy activities can be both physical and mental. For some people, a telephone call to their mother might be a breeze, a low energy activity, for others it might be very stressful and draining, a high energy activity.

Green	$\rightarrow$	Low energy
Orange	$\rightarrow$	Medium energy
Red	$\rightarrow$	High energy

Guide for interpreting your own activity diary

A lot of red and a little orange or green

This may indicate that you are doing too much during the week. Is there any way you could reduce your level of activity? Can someone else take on some of your activities? Is there time set aside for you during your week? Can you fit some 'pleasure activities' into your week?

A lot of green and a little red

Perhaps you are doing too little during your week. It is best not to increase your level of activity by a large amount in one go. Try to add an extra activity into your week, bit by bit—this will help you to see whether the extra activity is too much and leads you to 'bust' (see below).

Bunches of reds and bunches of greens

A pattern like this indicates that you may be 'booming and busting' (see below). Can you spread out your reds? A balanced day would be red-orange-green, red-orange-green, etc. This may not be possible all the time, but the more you can do it, the better.

Boom and bust

This describes a pattern of activity where you do too much (booming) when you are feeling 'OK', leading to a flare-up of your symptoms ('busting'). This pattern of behaviour is absolutely understandable. Many people become frustrated with the way their CFS/ME affects their life, so when an often rare 'good day' comes along, they try to get as much use out of it as possible. This often means over-activity however, often leading to an intensification of their symptoms.

Activity questionnaire

Do I need to increase my level activity?

Yes ☐

No ☐

Do I need to decrease my level of activity?

Yes ☐

No ☐

Do I need to balance my activities?

Yes ☐

No ☐

If you have answered yes to any of the questions above, note down steps that you can take to address these issues. For example, you may try to obtain balance in your activities by dividing the activity into smaller chunks and interspersing the chunks with a rest period (e.g. if the activity is cleaning the kitchen, you might want to consider washing the dishes first, taking a rest, drying and putting away the dishes, taking a rest, cleaning the work tops, taking a rest, cleaning the floor, taking a rest, etc). If you live in shared accommodation it may be helpful to discuss the steps with housemates.

Activity plan

CHAPTER SIX

Energy capsules

It might be helpful for you to think of your activities in terms of energy capsules. An energy capsule is an activity that you can do without worsening your symptoms. Energy capsules are time-limited. It may be that you can sit and browse the internet for 20 minutes without worsening your symptoms. It may be that if you try and do the same thing for an extra 10 minutes you end up feeling much worse.

Energy capsules come in three 'flavours'—mental, physical and restorative. Try, when you can, to take the capsules in alternative flavours. So you might take a mental energy capsule, followed by a restorative energy capsule, and then a physical energy capsule.

Rest(oration) does not mean sleeping, or even sitting on the sofa watching TV. For some people, even on a good day, watching TV can be a draining activity. Rest(oration) means relaxing, which means doing something that does not use up any of your energy, but may even replenish some of your energy stores. Some may find sitting quietly restorative, whilst others may have learnt some relaxation techniques that could count as rest.

Example energy capsules

Surfing the internet for 20 minutes	Reading novel for 50 minutes
15 minute walk to local shop	Working on coursework for 40 minutes
30 minute phonecall to friend	Watching television for 1 hour

Designing your own energy capsules can help you to avoid a boom and bust cycle. It also can provide you with a foundation level of activity that does not worsen your symptoms. Later, as you gain confidence in coping with your CFS/ME, you can think about gradually increasing the number of energy capsules that you have in any one day. This might mean that you are able to achieve more without feeling worse.

First, work out energy capsules for all of the activities that you regularly engage in, remembering to make a note of the 'flavour' of the capsule. Then work out how many capsules you can 'prescribe' yourself per day, without making your symptoms worse. This process initially may be one of trial and error, but once you find your correct dosage, and have adjusted to it, you can think about upping the number of capsules you take by one a day.

CHAPTER SEVEN

Impact crosses

We have spent some time looking at sleep and activity, and we hope that by now you are already experimenting with changes in your daily activities and trying out strategies that may help improve the quality of your sleep. Now we would like to return to a topic that we introduced in the third chapter (thoughts and feelings). Hopefully after completing your thoughts and feelings diaries, you will have seen that a relationship exists between how you think and how you feel. We want to expand on this relationship by looking at behaviour and physiology, as well as thoughts and feelings. To help understand what is going on, we will use impact crosses (sometimes called Hot Cross Buns).

An impact cross is just a visual representation or diagram to help us understand the interaction between how we think, how we feel, our behaviour and our physiology.

At this point, we would like to remind you of a bit of terminology we mentioned earlier. In the impact cross below, the term 'cognitions' means thoughts, and 'physiology' refers to what is happening physically and chemically in the body. In the example below, we can interpret the impact cross by saying that the thought 'I will never recover from this illness' has an

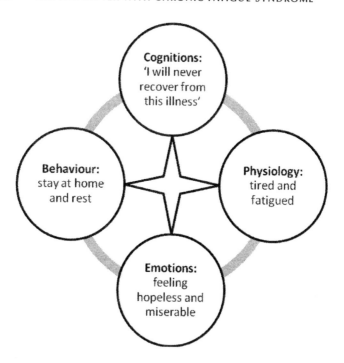

emotional consequence, i.e. the individual feels hopeless and miserable. This emphasises that there is a relationship between how we think and how we feel.

It is likely that when we feel hopeless and miserable, we will also feel lethargic and fatigued. So, if the individual is thinking that they will never recover from their illness, and is feeling hopeless, miserable, tired, and fatigued, it is likely that they will stay at home and rest. The behaviour of staying at home and resting might make the thought that they will never recover from their illness more believable.

In a way, we can see this thought or cognition as a 'self-fulfilling prophecy': i.e. the thought is likely to add to the individual's CFS/ME symptoms. Just to be make it absolutely clear at this point, we are not suggesting that CFS/ME is all about feeling sad or miserable. We are, however, saying that the thoughts that lead to these emotional states are not beneficial and are likely to result in an intensification of the symptoms of CFS/ME.

Let's look at another example, this time taking one of the entries from the thoughts and feelings diary in Chapter 3.

Situation: *Emma calls to invite me to meet for a coffee, but I am feeling very tired and I have to turn her down.*

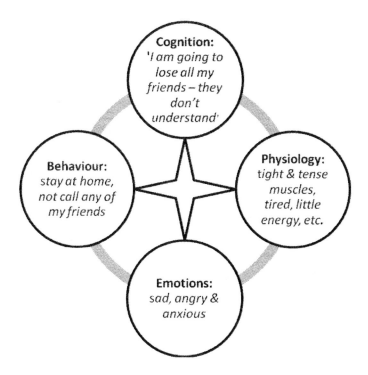

The impact cross above illustrates how certain unhelpful thoughts can lead to unhelpful behaviours, negative emotional states and unpleasant physiological reactions. This is important not just because it results in individuals feeling bad emotionally, but also because often people with CFS/ME report that when they feel stressed, their symptoms increase in intensity.

Unhelpful thoughts can lead to unhelpful behaviours which can end up leaving people stuck where they are, or even exacerbating the situation in which they find themselves. In the example above, Emma believes that she will lose her friends, and that her friends don't understand CFS/ME. The behavioural response of not calling her friends is likely to make her concerns true (another self-fulfilling prophecy)—she will lose all her friends, not because of the illness, but because she does not call them.

Situation: *I have arranged to meet Simon for a meal at a restaurant this Saturday.*

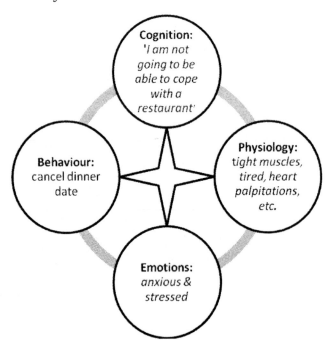

Of course, it may not be possible at the moment to go out with your friends all of the time, or to spend hours on the telephone without making your symptoms worse. However, if you were to use some of the strategies and tools we are looking at in this book (e.g. balancing activity, using energy capsules, etc) it may be possible to have some contact with your friends. You might be able to make an 'energy capsule phone call' of 10 minutes. While this may not be ideal, it may help to keep your friendships going until you are able to do more.

Now, using entries from your thoughts and feelings diary complete your own impact crosses. It may help if you discuss this with friends and family.

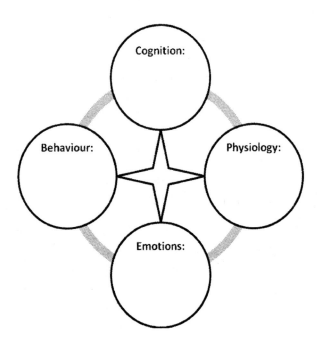

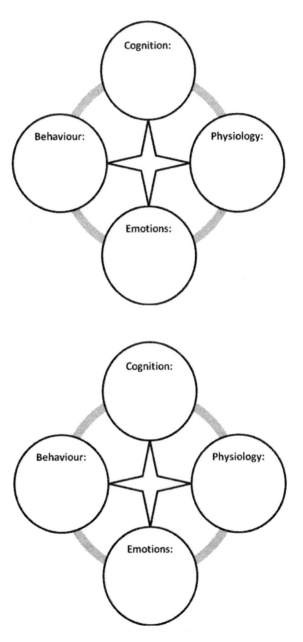

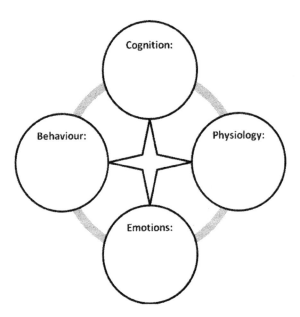

CHAPTER EIGHT

Challenging unhelpful patterns of thinking

After completing some impact crosses you will have seen how unhelpful patterns of thinking and behaviour can lead to negative emotions and unpleasant physiological responses. The earlier chapters dealt with suggesting new behaviours aimed at helping you manage your CFS/ME as well as reducing the severity of your symptoms. Now we are going to look at ways of changing problematic patterns of thinking.

The first step to changing negative automatic thoughts is to identify them. Hopefully, after the weeks that you have spent completing your thoughts and feelings diary, and creating impact crosses, this is a skill at which you have become proficient. We are now going to look at how to begin the process of modifying unhelpful thoughts.

At some point, our thinking becomes negatively-biased through making thinking errors. The more thinking errors we make, the more likely it is that our thinking will be unhelpful, which will have consequences on how we behave and how we feel, both emotionally and physically.

There are several ways of looking at how thinking may become negatively-biased. We have listed what we think are the most common ones below. We have even tried to construct a 'cheesy' acronym around them to make them easier to remember. Please read through the list on the next page and familiarize yourself with each one.

Part of the process of challenging negative automatic thoughts is to reduce how much you believe in them. You might find that this process is helped by learning the ways in which thinking can be negatively-biased. You then may be able to see if a particular thought that you have had shares characteristics with these thinking errors. Being able to see this may reduce how strongly you believe in any unhelpful thought. If you are able to do this, you might be able to reduce how strongly you experience any negative emotional or physical feeling that the unhelpful thought might cause. As you have seen from completing impact crosses, this may also have an effect on your behaviour, and perhaps on your CFS/ME symptoms.

Mind the GAAAP

Generalization: Drawing a conclusion about one situation based on another. E.g. you miss the bus and say to yourself, 'I am always late'

Attention: Includes focusing your attention on one aspect of a situation, or filtering out other pieces of information that might contradict your negative belief. E.g. you don't get the grade you want in an exam and say to yourself, 'I am a failure', ignoring all the exams that you have passed and other areas of your life where you are successful. The result of this is that unhelpful negative beliefs are reinforced.

Assumption: Making assumptions when you have not got enough information to be sure of your interpretation of the situation. An example might be assuming that you know what somebody else is thinking about you, or assuming that you know somebody else's motivation for saying or doing something (mind reading): e.g. he said he did not want to go out tonight because he does not want to spend time with me.

All-or-nothing thinking: This involves seeing the world, the people in it, and ourselves as either all good or all bad. It can result in catastrophising. E.g. You have a disagreement with a friend, and conclude that they don't like you anymore.

Prediction: This refers to when we believe we know how something will turn out. Of course, sometimes our predictions might turn out to be correct. However, we are often wrong as we cannot predict the future. Moreover, sometimes our beliefs about the future can become 'self-fulfilling prophecies'. An example might be if we believe we might not be able to cope with some task, we may avoid it—ensuring, therefore, that we do not cope with it!

Identifying thinking errors

Now that you are familiar with thinking errors, read through the following vignettes and try to identify the thinking errors (i.e. Mind the GAAAP) and see if you can generate an alternative explanation.

It is difficult to challenge our own thoughts, perhaps because we are so close to them. The idea behind using these vignettes to try and identify thinking errors is that it gives you practice at applying these techniques at a distance—you are examining someone else's thoughts and not your own. If you get good at applying these techniques, it may make it easier to use them on your own thoughts.

We have provided three vignettes. We have worked through the first one to illustrate the process, but have left the last two for you to complete.

Vignette 1

> *On Sunday, Frank waits by his phone for his daughter to call. She always calls on Sundays and tells him about her week. She does not call all evening. Frank thinks, 'she does not care enough to remember to call her own father'. He feels angry and upset. He is still angry when he speaks to her the next day, and ends up shouting at his daughter and calling her selfish.*

Mind the GAAAP

Attention error
Assumption error

Alternative interpretations

She may have been tired and in bed.

She may have been out and left her mobile phone at home.

She may have been having a bad day, and did not want to upset her father by talking to him when she was feeling bad.

She normally calls every Sunday, which would seem to suggest that she does care about her father: 'one swallow does not make a spring.'

Vignette 2

> *Lisa goes to a dinner party with her boyfriend. The guests are sat around the table and everyone except Lisa is engaged in conversation including her boyfriend who is talking to the female host (Julie) of the dinner party. Lisa thinks, 'Nobody wants to*

talk to me, I must be really boring! Even my boyfriend is more interested in Julie that me!' She feels sad, worthless, angry and embarrassed. She tells her boyfriend than she is not feeling well, and wants to leave the party early. On the way home, she argues with her boyfriend, accusing him of flirting with Julie.

Mind the GAAAP

Alternative interpretations

Vignette 3

Roger has suffered from CFS/ME for several years. On a good day, he decides that he will clean the house from top to bottom. Half way through he begins to feel very fatigued and symptomatic. He thinks, 'here it goes again, I can't do anything anymore.' He feels depressed and hopeless. He goes back to bed and rests for two days.

Mind the GAAAP

Alternative interpretations

Your own use of thinking errors

Now look through the thoughts and feelings diaries and the impact crosses that you have completed. Can you identify whether you have used any of the thinking errors from the list above? Again, if there is somebody that you trust and you are having trouble identifying any thinking errors in your thoughts, perhaps you could ask their advice and to look over your list.

Alternative thoughts

When we have an unhelpful thought it is very challenging to see things any other way. We tend to accept thoughts as facts—accurate reflections of reality. However, this is rarely the case—our thoughts are just one possible interpretation of a situation.

It may be challenging to generate alternative thoughts, but it is not impossible, and with practice it becomes easier. Experimental psychology has shown that when a specific behaviour is rewarded, it is more likely to occur again. It is possible to assume that the same process occurs with our thinking. Perhaps, if a more helpful thought is rewarded with a positive emotion or physiological reaction, or with a more helpful behaviour, then maybe this new way of thinking might be more likely to occur again. Eventually, the alternative, more helpful way of thinking could become the 'automatic thought'.

One of the reasons it might be difficult to generate an alternative thought may be because you believe in the original thought very strongly. If you try to just stop thinking an unhelpful thought, the chances are you will think it even more—just like if you try to stop an annoying tune running through your head. Perhaps a more effective way of getting yourself in a position where you can generate alternative thoughts is to try and weaken your belief in the original unhelpful thought.

The immediate goal is NOT to stop all negative thoughts, but to reduce how strongly you believe in them and therefore change how you respond to them. We all have negative unhelpful thoughts—what gives them the power to affect us is how strongly we believe them. We might have thought such as 'I am loser', but if we don't believe it, it is likely that we won't be affected by it. Thoughts are not facts.

Taking the iTEST

You may find it helpful to challenge your unhelpful thoughts before you generate alternative thoughts. The iTest may help you remember the ways in which you can do this. It is (yet another) acronym. This one is designed to prompt you to ask a series of questions about the negative thought. If you try to ask yourself as many of these questions as are relevant to your thought, then this process might help to weaken your strength of belief in the unhelpful negative thought.

iTest

Ignore	Are you **ignoring** or dismissing information that might contradict the unhelpful thought?
Time:	Is the unhelpful thought true all of the **time**? If it isn't, this might mean that unhelpful thought does not reflect what is really going on.
Evidence:	What is the **evidence** for and against the unhelpful thought? It is important to be fair, and to argue the thought from both sides. It may be time to 'Take Your Thought to Court' (see below).
Someone else:	What would you say to **someone else** if they expressed the unhelpful thought to you? Or what would someone else say to you if they knew you had this thought, e.g. a friend?
Tally	**Tally** up the advantages and disadvantages of the unhelpful thought.

Hopefully, the questions that the iTest prompt you to ask are, on the whole, quite straightforward. We will explain the iTest in a little more depth over the next couple of pages.

Take your thought to court

This is about weighing up the evidence that supports and contradicts your unhelpful thought. We change our minds about things in everyday life when we consider new bits of information. For example, we may meet someone socially and our first impression is that the individual is quiet and moody. Later on however, we may find out that the person has just separated from their partner. This bit of information may lead us to re-evaluate our beliefs about that individual.

We are not always going to have all of the information available to us all of the time, and it is essential to realise how this might affect our interpretations. We should at least make sure we are considering all of the information that we have available. Believing that something is true does not necessarily make it true—i.e. would thoughts stand up in court?

Taking your thought to court requires that you consider the evidence for and against a thought being realistic or not realistic.

Example

Situation: *Turn down an invite for coffee with friends as feeling too tired*
Thought: *I am going to lose all of my friends because of this illness*

Evidence for	Evidence against
• *I have not been out with friends for 3 months* • *Beverley no longer calls me*	• *My friends continue to ask me out* • *Emma, Nathan, and Rachel still phone* • *When I invited Rachel to come to my flat for a coffee, she accepted*

Tally the advantages and disadvantages

This is the last bit left to do of the iTEST. Once you have challenged your unhelpful thought, it is important to consider the advantages and disadvantages of it. This is vital, because if we believe thinking in a certain way is beneficial, it is going to be very hard to think in a different way.

Example

Situation: *Turn down an invite for coffee with friends as feeling too tired*

Thought: *I am going to lose all of my friends because of this illness*

Advantages	Disadvantages
It might prepare me for losing my friends It may encourage me to go out more	It makes me stressed It might make me go out when I am not feeling good enough It might make me behave in an unfriendly manner to my friends, therefore driving them away

Taking the iTEST

On the following page is an example of an iTEST sheet that might help you put all of these techniques together. Remember, that your goal in using these techniques is to reduce how much you believe in the unhelpful thought. After the example iTEST sheet, there is a blank version for you to use.

As with most things in life, the more you practice the better you will become at the iTEST technique. At first, it is likely that this will feel unnatural and uncomfortable, but through repetition of the technique, it should eventually become automatic, and you will no longer need to be completing iTEST sheets. Remember that you may also have to use the thought chain technique described in chapter 3 to identify the underlying negative thought.

Example iTEST

Date	Situation	Thought (rate strength of belief in thought out of 100%)	Feeling (rate intensity of feeling out of 100%)
15/8/09	*Friends invite me to dinner in a res- taurant on Friday.*	*I won't be able to cope with a restaurant, and I will have to let down my friends. My friends will stop inviting me out (80%)*	*Anxious, stressed & depressed (65%)*

Ignore	Are you ignoring or dismissing information that might contradict the unhelpful thought?

I was able to cope last time—I did feel fatigued afterwards, but it did not lead to a major setback. Even though I have had to turn my friends down before, they still call and invite me out.

Time	Is the unhelpful thought true all of the time?

When I feel better I feel more able to cope. Also, other times I know that my friends understand that I am ill, and would not stop liking me just because I have to cancel a dinner date.

Evidence	Taking your thought to court

Evidence for	Evidence against
I have been ill for years and I know that sometimes I just don't have the energy to do things.	*I was able to meet friends in a café last week. My friends still call me and invite me out.*

Someone else	What would you says to someone else if they expressed the unhelpful thought to you?

I would tell them at this point they don't know how they are going to feel on Friday. I would also tell them that I would not stop being their friend if they were ill and had to cancel on me.

T_{ally}	Tally up the advantages and disadvantages of the unhelpful thought.

Advantages	Disadvantages
It will prepare me for having to turn people down. I can let my friends know earlier.	It will mean I worry which makes me feel more stressed and less able to cope. It might mean that I don't go out when I feel ok.

Alternative thought

I may or may not be able to go out. I don't know yet! My friends will not judge me harshly for cancelling.

Re-rate strength of belief in original unhelpful thought	40%

Re-rate strength of original feeling	45%

iTEST

Date	Situation	Thought (rate strength of belief in thought out of 100%)	Feeling (rate intensity of feeling out of 100%)

I_{gnore}	Are you ignoring or dismissing information that might contradict the unhelpful thought?

T_{ime}	Is the unhelpful thought true all of the time?

$E_{vidence}$	Taking your thought to court	
Evidence for		*Evidence against*

$S_{omeone\ else}$	What would you says to someone else if they expressed the unhelpful thought to you?

T_{ally}	Tally up the advantages and disadvantages of the unhelpful thought.	
Advantages		*Disadvantages*

Alternative thought

Re-rate strength of belief in original unhelpful thought

Re-rate strength of original feeling

After attempting the iTEST, look back at how strongly you rated your belief in your original unhelpful thought and how you rated your strength of feeling. Has this rating changed now you have taken the iTEST? If you have reduced your strength of belief in your negative thought, and reduced the strength of your negative feeling, then it would seem that the iTEST is working for you.

The process of changing thoughts requires time and repetition. Through practicing the iTEST, you may be able to reduce the impact that unhelpful thoughts have on your behaviour, emotions and physiological state.

CHAPTER NINE

Stress and anxiety

Stress and anxiety are common problems that nearly all of us will experience at some point of our lives. What happens to your CFS/ME symptoms when you become stressed? Do they become more intense? The symptoms of stress and anxiety can be very powerful in their own right, for people with and without CFS/ME.

Some of the symptoms of stress and anxiety:

- Increased heart rate/palpitations
- Trembling/hand tremor
- Dry throat and mouth
- Sleep difficulties
- Butterflies in stomach
- Shortness of breath
- Pins and needles
- Racing thoughts
- Difficulties with concentration

Many studies have shown that stress can impact on your immune system in a powerful way, altering normal functioning of the immune system. This is discussed in Chapter 13.

Fight or flight response

When we are in a dangerous situation, our bodies respond by readying ourselves to fight or run away from (flight) the situation. The body achieves this state by releasing hormones called adrenaline and noradrenaline. Adrenaline and noradrenaline produce all of the symptoms of stress (and anxiety). These symptoms all enhance our ability to survive dangerous situations. One example is that adrenaline enables our muscles to work more powerfully so that we can run faster or punch harder.

The flight or fight response is vital for our survival. Problems occur when it gets triggered inappropriately, when we are not in a life or death situation. This can happen when we appraise or interpret a situation as being extreme in a stressful or anxiety-provoking way.

Example

Situation	*Deadline for big project approaching at work*
Thought	*If I do not finish in time, I could lose my job.*
	If I do not make a perfect job of the project, I will lose the respect of my work colleagues.
Emotion	*Anxiety/Stress*
Physiological symptoms	*Tiredness, headaches, heart palpitations, etc.*

You might find it useful to distinguish between stress and anxiety by looking at the intensity of your symptoms. Anxiety can be thought of resulting in more intense physiological symptoms that happen in relatively brief period of time.

Stress	*Anxiety*
Goes on for a long period of time	Brief
Perceived danger to occur at some point in the future	Perceived danger immediate

Stress

We experience stress when we believe that we do not have the capabilities to cope or deal with situation in which we find ourselves.

Sometimes we may not have the ability to deal with the situation in which we find ourselves; other times we just *believe* that we don't have this ability. Whichever the case, we may worry about the consequences of not being able to deal with the situation. Worry itself is a cognitively demanding activity—meaning that it takes up a lot of our mental resources, reducing the resources (our ability) left to deal with the situation or come up with solutions to problems, as well as being mentally fatiguing in its own right.

Many people with CFS/ME have noticed that when they become stressed, their symptoms become worse. So it is important to try and find ways to reduce the stress we experience. When you find yourself stressed, it might be helpful to ask yourself the following questions:

1. Have I got the resources to cope with this situation, or do I just believe that I have not?
2. Am I worrying? Worrying can exacerbate stress.
3. Do I need to try and change the situation or change my thinking?

It is difficult to answer the first question if you are worrying, so we will look at ways of dealing with worry first.

Worry

Worry is a strategy for thinking. We are worrying when we dwell on a certain thought or concern over and over again. This has the effect of keeping our bodies in the fight or flight mode and therefore maintaining the symptoms of stress and anxiety.

Components of worry
Circular thinking: the same thoughts over and over again
Anticipation of a negative outcome to some future event

Situation	*Deadline for big project approaching at work*
Thought	*If I do not finish in time, I could lose my job.* *If I do not make a perfect job of the project, I will lose the respect of my work colleagues.*
Thinking strategy	*Worry about the big project*
Emotion	*Anxiety/Stress*
Physiological symptoms	*Tiredness, headaches, heart palpitations, difficulty sleeping etc*

Techniques for dealing with worry and stress

Here are some simple strategies and tools that might help you deal with your worry and stress.

Talk it over:	Talk with friends and family about what is stressing you. Speaking to other people can provide you with a different perspective on what is troubling you.
Relaxation:	Try any relaxation techniques that you have learnt.
Set realistic goals:	If your goals are unrealistic, then this is likely to increase your worry and stress. Use the SMART goal setting technique to help you plan and choose your goals.
Worry record:	Write down your worrying thoughts. This may help turn them from a circular thinking process to a linear thinking process (i.e. with a beginning and an end).

Worry period: Set aside at set period of half an hour each day to worry. Ensure that it is the same time each day. If you find yourself worrying outside of your worry period, make an note of what you are worrying about in your worry record, and say to yourself, 'I have noted my worry in my worry record so I won't forget it, and I shall postpone my worry to my worry period.

Positive and negative beliefs about worry

Often people have positive and negative beliefs about worry. It is thought that these beliefs result in people beginning to worry, and in maintaining worry once it has begun.

Positive beliefs about worry

> *'Worrying about something helps me to prepare for future problems'*
> *'Worrying helps me cope'*
> *'Worrying helps me to solve problems'*

Negative beliefs about worry

> *'Worrying could make me go mad'*
> *'My worry is uncontrollable'*

Take a moment now to note down some more advantages and disadvantages to worrying. Rate how strongly you believe in each advantage and disadvantage. It might be helpful to use the above examples of positive and negative beliefs to start you off.

Advantages of worry	Disadvantages of worry

We shall view what you perceive to be the advantages and disadvantages to worry as being your positive and negative beliefs about worry. The diagram below describes a simplified model of worry that is usually applied in the treatment of Generalised Anxiety Disorder, a psychological disorder characterised by excessive worry. Even though it has been developed for more extreme cases, it might help you to understand your worry.

The idea is that when we are faced with a situation or event that we perceive as negative, we experience a negative emotional state. This is just like what we have been doing in chapter 3 when we were looking at thoughts and feelings. The model goes on to suggest that, because of our positive beliefs about worry (i.e. what we think are the advantages to worry) we try to cope with the negative emotion by worrying—we believe that worry will help. However, by worrying we just end up feeling more anxious and stressed.

At the same time, when we start to worry, our negative beliefs about worry are activated (i.e. what we think are the disadvantages to worry). This just gives us more to worry about, and further increases our stress and anxiety.

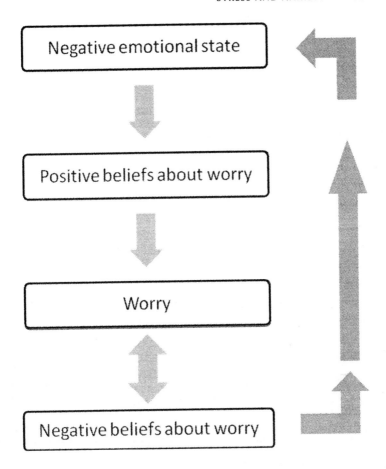

Studies suggest that if people challenge their positive and negative beliefs about worry, then they might worry less, and consequently experience less stress and anxiety. You have learnt a tool for challenging unhelpful thoughts such as your positive and negative beliefs about worry from working through this book. We are going to adapt the iTEST and use it to challenge positive and negative beliefs about worry.

Belief about worry	
My worry is uncontrollable (90%)	

I_{gnore}	Are you ignoring or dismissing information that might contradict the unhelpful thought?

I was worrying yesterday about getting back to work. Then a friend called at my house unexpectedly, and she had brought round a DVD of a film I have wanted to see for ages. This seemed to stop me from worrying.

T_{ime}	Is the unhelpful thought true all of the time?

There are times when I can disrupt and stop my worrying.

$E_{vidence}$	Taking your thought to court

Evidence for	*Evidence against*
Once I start worrying it is difficult to stop. Last week I could not get to sleep because I was worrying so much.	*I have managed to keep my worry to my 'worry period', which means I have some control over it. If I am distracted, my mind stops worrying.*

$S_{omeone\ else}$	What would you says to someone else if they expressed the unhelpful thought to you?

I would point out the times when they have been able to stop worrying.

T_{ally}	Tally up the advantages and disadvantages of the unhelpful thought.

Advantages	*Disadvantages*
I can't think of any!	*It means that I end up worrying more and feeling more stressed.*

Alternative belief

I can control my worry some of the time.

Re-rate strength of original belief	*50%*

Now try the same with all of your own positive and negative beliefs about worry. Remember, your goal is to try and reduce how strongly you hold these beliefs.

Belief about worry	
Ignore	Are you ignoring or dismissing information that might contradict the unhelpful thought?

Time	Is the unhelpful thought true all of the time?

Evidence	Taking your thought to court	
Evidence for		*Evidence against*
Someone else	What would you says to someone else if they expressed the unhelpful thought to you?	

Tally	Tally up the advantages and disadvantages of the unhelpful thought.	
Advantages		*Disadvantages*

Alternative belief

Re-rate strength of original belief

Stop signals

One common negative belief about worry is that some people believe that it is uncontrollable. However, we suggest that it is not uncontrollable, it is just that the goal for worrying is unattainable, therefore people who believe that worry is uncontrollable rarely get the signal to stop worrying—i.e. that they have achieved their goal. Some people believe that worrying might help them solve some problem in the future. How do they know if they have solved the problem and achieved their goal in worrying? If the problem is in future, do they have to wait till it occurs to know if they have solved it? Do they believe that they know they have solved the problem when they feel less anxious and stressed? This is where the problem lies. If your signal to stop worrying is when you feel less anxious, but worrying just increases your stress and anxiety, you are never going to get the signal to stop worrying.

What tells you that you have worried enough, and you can stop worrying? What is your goal in worrying? Is it to make you prepared for the problem in future? If so, how do you know you are prepared? In other words, what tells you to stop worrying? If you are not getting a stop signal, it could be very difficult to halt your worry and it may result in your worry seeming uncontrollable.

We are going to look at a technique that might help you reduce your worry by transforming it into a goal. By having a goal with a clear objective, you might also end up with a clear and achievable stop signal.

Reframing a worry as a goal

This is a technique for shifting from worry to problem-solving thinking. Worry seems to increase stress, and doesn't help you achieve your goals. Reframing your worry as a goal may help you figure out whether you can cope or deal with the situation you find yourself in. It also can help you to plan how to change stressful situations.

This technique has a clear stop signal—i.e. when you have planned to achieve the goal.

1. **Identify** what is stressing you. Ask yourself exactly what is it about the stressor which is concerning you.
2. **Reframe** what is stressing you as a goal.
3. **Plan** to achieve that goal.

Example of reframing technique

Identify stressor: *A big electricity bill lands of your doorstep. I am concerned that I cannot pay it.*

Reframing: *Pay the electricity bill*

Plan:
Phone electricity company to see about spreading the payments
Agree a payment plan
Budget to meet plan

Exercise

Now try and use the reframing technique in the example below.

Identify stressor: *Your daughter has fallen behind in her school work.*
Reframing:

Plan:

Now try to use the technique with some of your worries or stressors.

Identify stressor:
Reframing:

Plan:

Acute anxiety or panic

When the fight or flight response is triggered in a short episode, we usually call this 'anxiety'. When it is triggered and lasts for a longer period, we usually call this 'stress'.

Sometimes, our fight or flight response is triggered in the most unusual and unexpected situations: for example, when in a supermarket, or when driving in a car, or even when we are just sat on the sofa watching TV.

There is usually some thought that triggers the fight or flight response, though sometimes we may not be fully aware of the thought (it can be an **automatic thought**). The thought tends to be anxiety-provoking and is about perceiving the situation or event as dangerous, which triggers the flight or response. The fight or flight response results in various physiological changes occurring in the body—and if you are not aware that they are due to adrenaline and noradrenalin, they can be anxiety-provoking in their own right. In episodes of acute anxiety, these bodily sensations due to the fight or flight response can be misinterpreted as being dangerous. This, in turn, results in more anxiety, and a more intense fight or flight response.

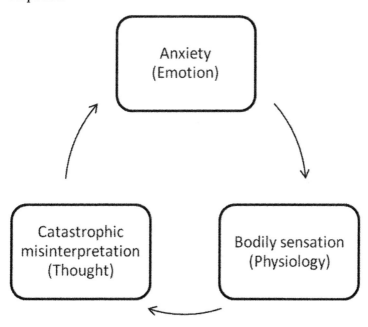

So imagine that you are sat there on the sofa, or queuing in a shop, when all of a sudden you experience these strange symptoms. If you did not know that they were just normal adrenaline effects, you might misinterpret these symptoms as meaning that something very bad was happening to you: e.g. 'I am having a heart attack'. 'I am going mad', 'I am going to collapse', etc. These misinterpretations will trigger the release of more adrenaline, thereby increasing the symptoms. These anxiety symptoms can seem to reinforce the thought that something bad is going to happen to us (e.g. heart palpitations may indeed seem to support the idea that we are about to have a panic attack).

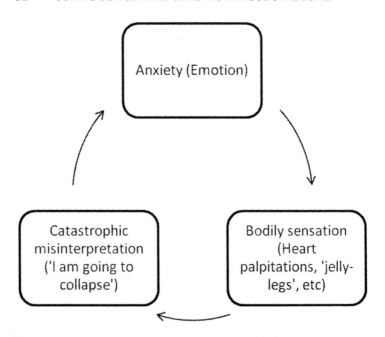

These intense acute anxiety episodes can be very unpleasant experiences and lead us to avoiding these situations in future. However, by avoiding the situations in which we experienced these episodes, we never teach ourselves that they are not actually dangerous, and this therefore maintains our anxiety. Avoiding situations because we believe that we cannot cope with them can mean that our belief becomes a self-fulfilling prophecy.

If you experience chest pain, or pain in your arm, it is important that you get this checked out by a doctor before you attribute this to anxiety.

What can help if you experience an acute anxiety episode?

- Understanding the vicious cycle of panic (above) may help us not to misinterpret the normal symptoms of the fight or flight response.

- Tell yourself 'these are just normal effects of adrenaline— nothing dangerous is actually happening to me'.
- Try to focus your attention on something external to your body, and not on your internal bodily symptoms. For example, if you were in a supermarket queue, you could count the number of people with blonde hair, or how many lights are on the ceilings, or focus your attention on the sounds of the cars outside.
- Try to identify the automatic thought that triggered the anxiety, and take the iTEST.

CHAPTER TEN

Core beliefs

So far in this book we have looked at the relationship between thoughts, feelings, behaviour, and physiology. It is now time to revisit the vulnerability factors that you identified in chapter 1. We are going to look at these factors to work out whether they still have an impact on you today. In doing so, we need to look at core beliefs and rules for living.

A core belief is a particular type of thought of which we might not be consciously aware. Such thoughts govern how we view the world, and therefore can affect our cognitions, feelings, behaviours and physiology. One of the fundamental ideas behind this concept is that we interpret and perceive the world around us based in part on what we already know.

What we see depends on what we already know

We acquire our core beliefs through our experiences in life. For example, imagine that you are on a platform at a station as a train arrives. The train casts a larger and larger image on the retina at the back of your eyes as it moves towards the platform. If the only source of information by which we make sense of our experiences was received through our senses (e.g. through our eyes), how would you know whether the train was getting closer, or whether the train was growing larger? Our experiences have taught us that trains stay the same size, and from this we can deduce that if the train is not getting larger, it must be getting closer. This illustrates one of our common core beliefs, that of size consistency.

It might come as a relief that the belief that trains stay the same size is not the only thing that we learn in life. Throughout lives, and perhaps especially in our childhood, we are taught a variety of beliefs, some passed on to us by our parents, others by friends, and others still by all the different experiences to which we are exposed. We acquire beliefs about ourselves, the relationships we have with others, and the world around us. Sometimes, however, the beliefs that we learn are not always so helpful. They may have been useful at one stage in our lives, or they may have never besen useful to us at all.

This is not to say, however, that we do not need core beliefs. Core beliefs are mental 'short cuts' that help us to make sense of the world around us. The amount of information entering our brain, via our senses, at any one time is huge. To process all this information from 'scratch' (i.e. without core beliefs to help us make sense of the world) would be demanding in the extreme.

The problem with core beliefs, however, is that once they are moulded, it can be very difficult to change them—whether they are helpful or not. Such beliefs dictate how we see the world and, as with the example of the train approaching the station, we experience this perception as the truth. This tends to mean that we do not see or process experiences or information that does not fit in with our beliefs. This, in turn, means that our core beliefs do not have to change to adapt to new information because there is no new information to adapt to.

The example below illustrates how having two different core beliefs can result in having two very different interpretations of the same situation.

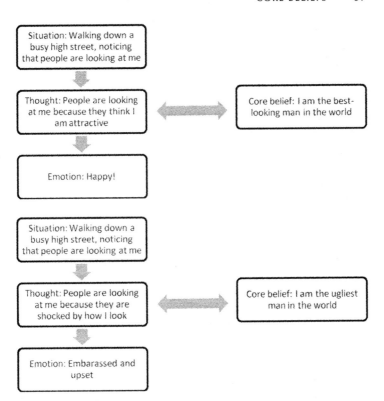

Core beliefs not only influence how we see the world around us, they also affect our behaviour. The way in which our core beliefs affect our behaviour tends to mean that we find ourselves in situations that provide information that reinforces our core beliefs.

Rules for living

In each life lived we are abide by our own personal rules for living. These rules govern how we behave in response to different situations. For example, one person might operate by the rule that they must always put others first. On the face of it, a rule like this might seem a perfectly good rule held by someone caring and empathic. Such a rule, however, may create problems. There are going to be occasions where we need to take care of own interests first, before we look out for others. Indeed, always putting other people first might mean that we neglect our own needs to such an extent that we are no longer able to care for others.

Rules for living, core beliefs and vulnerability factors are related concepts. We can look at them as three different ways of looking at the same thing: i.e. ourselves and our behaviour.

Vulnerability factors, rules for living and core beliefs

We are now going to see if any of the vulnerability factors that you previously identified coincide with your own rules for living. First, we will look at Vincent, the self-employed builder we described in Chapter 1. He seemed to be a perfectionist, insofar as he 'always' wanted to produce work to the 'highest standard'. From this, we are going to deduce a rule for living based on this vulnerability factor. It seems to us that Vincent is governed by a rule like 'I must always produce work to a perfect standard'.

Now it is time to figure out the advantages and disadvantages of such a rule for living. We will illustrate how to do this in the tables below.

Rule for living

I must always produce work to a perfect standard

Advantages	Disadvantages
I always do my best and I get a sense of achievement.	*It is exhausting.*
People are impressed with what I do and it helps me develop a good reputation.	*I get stressed and angry with myself when I fail to reach my own standards.*

Remember Anna, the woman who had the 'messy' divorce and spends her weekends looking after her mother, also from chapter 1? She might have a rule like 'I should always put others before me'. Let's look at the advantages and disadvantages of such a rule.

Rule for living

I should always put others before me

Advantages	Disadvantages
I make sure that everybody around is ok, which makes me feel good.	*It is exhausting and sometimes I don't have the energy left to look out for others.*
It makes the world a nicer place!	*It means that sometimes my needs are not met, and I am left feeling upset.*
People appreciate me for caring for them.	

Can you deduce your own rules for living from the vulnerability factors you identified in chapter 1? Try to work them out and fill in the table below.

Rule for living

Advantages	Disadvantages

Now look at your own rules for living. Do the disadvantages outweigh the advantages? Do you think that the disadvantages might contribute to your CFS/ME? Remember when we looked at maintaining factors in Chapter 1—do any of the disadvantages result in over-activity or inactivity, or affect your mood negatively, or increase how stressed you feel, or contribute to your symptoms in any other way? Do your own rules for living help or hinder your management of, and recovery from, CFS/ME?

Perhaps you have decided that your own rules for living are hindering your recovery from CFS/ME. Maybe you have decided that they are not, either way, it might be interesting to figure out your core belief, or beliefs, that underlie your own rules for living. To do this, we suggest using the 'thought chain' tool that we described in chapter 3. The question that we

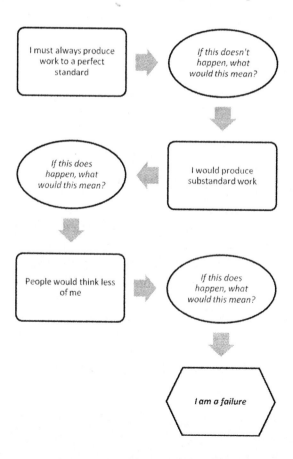

are going to use to forge the links in the chain is *'If this does or doesn't happen, what would this mean?'* To illustrate this, we will use Vincent's rule for living.

So it seems that one of Vincent's core beliefs is that he is 'a failure'. He would know best whether this was one of his core beliefs, simply by asking himself whether the belief feels true for him. Now try this technique to identify your own core beliefs. After you have generated some possible core beliefs, ask yourself how strongly you believe in them. Perhaps rate them with a percentage, so that a rating of 100% would mean that you totally believe in the core belief, whereas 0% would mean that you don't believe it at all.

Other ways to identify core beliefs

Identifying core beliefs can be a difficult task as we are rarely conscious of these thoughts; nonetheless it is possible. We suggest two methods which may help you to identify your own core beliefs.

Looking for themes in your unhelpful thoughts diary

Date	Situation	Thought (rate strength of belief in thought out of 100%)	Feeling (rate intensity of feeling out of 100%)
25/2/09	*Emma calls to invite me to meet for a coffee, but I am feeling very tired and I have to turn her down*	*I am going to lose all my friends because of this illness (70%)*	*Sad (80%)*
	I find out that my friends had all gone out last Friday without telling me	*My friends do not like me anymore (60%)*	*Hopeless (90%)*
		I must be really boring (70%)	*Sad (80%)*

From the two thoughts in the preceding example, it would seem that a possible core belief might have something to do with friendships being fragile. Maybe the core belief is something like '*I am not worthy of friendship*' or '*If I don't spend lots of time with my friends, I will lose them as friends*'.

Once you have identified some themes like this, ask yourself whether you agree with the core belief. How true does it feel for you? Again, rate, as a percentage, how strongly you believe in the core belief that you have identified.

The 'what does that mean if that is true?' technique

This technique also involves using your thoughts and feelings diary, impact crosses, and/or iTests. Take one of the unhelpful thoughts that you have identified previously, and keep asking yourself what it would mean if it was true.

Date	Situation	Thought (rate strength of belief in thought out of 100%)	Feeling (rate intensity of feeling out of 100%)
25/2/09	*Emma calls to invite me to meet for a coffee, but I am feeling very tired and I have to turn her down*	*I am going to lose all my friends because of this illness (70%)*	*Sad (80%)*

Modifying core beliefs

Modifying *unhelpful* core beliefs is difficult because these are held 'deep-down' and may have been affecting our thinking and behaviour for a long time. Changing core beliefs is made even more difficult because of their very nature. They tend to make us pay attention to things, and behave in certain

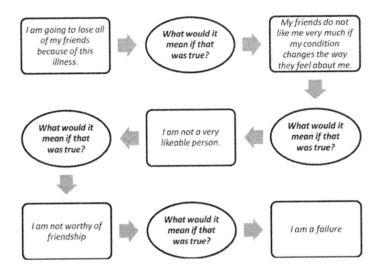

ways, that mean we tend to only ever have experiences which reinforce our core beliefs. Core beliefs are forced to change when we start to *process* (e.g. pay attention to) information that contradicts them.

The first step we can take in challenging core beliefs is figuring out exactly what we mean by them. If we have a core belief such as 'I am worthless', exactly what does 'worthless' mean? The term 'worthless' means different things to different people. Try to specify your own definition of, and criteria for, your core belief. This is a bit like devising the SMART goals from Chapter 2. If you can decide on a clear definition of your core belief and specify criteria by which you can measure it, you may be in a better position to challenge it.

The first step then, is to rate how strongly you believe in your core belief and then specify your definition of it. We encourage you to rate how strongly you believe in your core belief because it may help you work out which techniques are successful in modifying your core belief. The goal of this whole process is the same as your goal in challenging unhelpful negative thoughts: to reduce how strongly you believe in the core belief.

In the example below, we can see that the individual holds the belief that they are worthless very strongly. Think back to the impact crosses that we looked at in an earlier chapter and consider what an effect such a belief might have on an individual's behaviour, emotional state, and physiology.

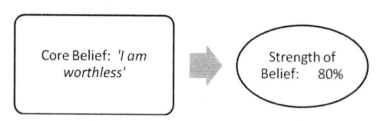

Also consider what you have read earlier in this chapter. How would an individual with such a core belief be likely to interpret their experiences and the world around them?

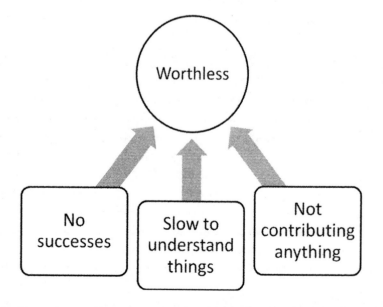

In the example above, the individual has identified 3 aspects to their definition of what being worthless means to them. Remember that the idea is that core beliefs determine how we interpret our experiences and the world around us. It is likely that an individual with such a core belief would ignore any successes that they have had, or any contributions that they have made, and focus on all the occasions where they may not have picked things up quite as quickly as they would have liked.

In order to change problematic core beliefs like the one above, we need to pay attention to information that we may have previously ignored. One way to do this is to think of things which would count as a success or a contribution. If you are trying to do this yourself, it may be helpful to conduct a mini-survey. What do other people count as a success or a contribution? You do not necessarily need to explain to them that you are working through a self-help book if you do not want to. You could simply say that you are curious as to what they think.

Example successes

- Passing an exam
- Dealing with or solving a problem
- Passing a driving test
- Writing a short-story

Example contributions

- Helping someone with a problem
- Raising a family
- Working as a team

The next step is like the 'taking your thought to court' technique described in chapter 8. In this case, you weigh up the evidence for and against you having experiences that match the examples you have generated. Remember, the goal here is to pay attention to information that you might normally ignore. Again, if there is somebody that you trust and who knows you well, perhaps ask them to help. They might be better able to think of evidence for you matching one of the examples than you. We shall use the example successes to illustrate.

Passing an exam

Evidence for	Evidence against
I got 4 GCSEs	I failed the rest of them because I had to miss a lot of time off school due to illness

Dealing with or solving a problem

Evidence for	Evidence against
My daughter had fallen behind in her school work, and I organised a meeting with her tutor. As a result extra tuition was arranged	I was unable to figure out how to use my new television

Hopefully, this should guide you to pay attention to information that contradicts the unhelpful core belief that you have identified. If it does not, perhaps you could use the goal setting technique described in Chapter 2 to provide you with new evidence. For example, if the individual with the core belief 'I am worthless' has *really* never passed an exam of any description, perhaps they could devise a SMART goal of passing an exam or test.

The other component to the example core belief we looked at above was that being slow to understand things means that you are worthless. This raises a few questions: (1) how slow to understand things do you need to be to be worthless, (2) how many things do you need to be slow to understand in order to be worthless, (3) is it true that you are slow to understand things, and finally, (4) would you apply this rule to other people?

How could the individual begin to answer the 4 questions above? Well, perhaps the individual could try using the iTest. They could enter in the thought 'I am slow to understand things' and test it. If they could challenge that thought, perhaps this would help to weaken the unhelpful core belief.

What we are trying to encourage you to do here is to challenge every aspect at every possible level of your unhelpful core belief. This is a process that requires a lot of effort and may involve a lot of different techniques taught in this book, as well as others that you have picked up elsewhere or have thought up yourself. However, if you think that your unhelpful core beliefs are having a major negative impact on your life, perhaps this will be effort well spent.

If you try this process and are able to identify a core belief that you would like to change, remember to re-rate your strength of belief in the core belief after you have gone through the process of challenging it. This will give you some idea as to whether this technique is working for you. Even if there is just a tiny shift, then this is positive. Hopefully a small shift in your strength of belief will give you enough motivation to persevere with this and the other techniques described in this book until you have attained your goals.

New beliefs

We hope that, by going through the processes described in this book, your strength of belief in your original negative core belief will have been weakened. After working through this process, you may want to start thinking about what core beliefs you would like to have. Make a note of these.

Perhaps take them through the same process that you have done with your unhelpful core beliefs (after all, it is only fair to treat them the same). Note down a new belief, rate who strongly you believe it, define the different aspects to it, specify different criteria for each aspect, and finally weigh up the evidence. Does your strength of belief in your new core belief become weaker or stronger?

CHAPTER ELEVEN

Symptom mapping

Learning to listen and understand your body

Some people with CFS/ME may be highly-motivated and 'driven' with characteristics that may verge on what might be called 'perfectionism'. Often, people with CFS/ME have pushed their bodies very hard at some point in their lives prior to acquiring the condition. For example, some individuals may have contracted a virus and been ill but continued to work long hours. This may not be true for all people with CFS/ME, but what seems to be quite common is that, at some point in their lives, people have stopped listening to, or have misunderstood, what their body was trying to tell them.

What are setbacks and relapses?

In this book, the terms setbacks and relapses mean the same thing. They refer to a sudden major increase the intensity of your symptoms. The next chapter deals with this aspect to the management of your CFS/ME in more detail.

Warning signs, recovery signs and natural responses

Once individuals acquire CFS/ME, it seems they try hard to listen to what their body is telling them, however it appears that the misunderstanding of what their body is saying persists. Some symptoms are signs that the body is recovering. For example, if you experience aches and pains after exercise but these symptoms do not lead to a setback, then these symptoms might mean that you are getting fitter. If you experience brain-fog after a poor night's sleep or after concentrating for a long time when you have not done so for a while, and these symptoms do not lead to a setback, then these symptoms could be considered a 'natural response': i.e. most people who have slept poorly and are not used to concentrating for a long period of time will experience confusion or feel muddled.

However, some symptoms will be warning signs. They will be your body's way of telling you that you have been overdoing it. These symptoms may result in a setback or relapse.

People who have had CFS/ME for any length of time often report a variety of different symptoms. It is rare that an individual has exactly the same pattern of symptoms as another. Symptoms will also mean different things and have different consequences to different people. Therefore, it is important to figure out what each symptom means to you and what the consequence of each symptom is for you.

Whether a symptom is a warning sign, a recovery sign or a natural response will depend on the consequence of the symptom. Symptom mapping can help you to figure out how best to respond to your symptoms, as well as helping to reduce how stressed your symptoms might make you feel. This is important because in our clinic many people with CFS/ME report that there is a relationship between how stressed they feel and the intensity of their symptoms. This might mean that if somebody tends interpret most of their symptoms as being warning signs, they might end-up feeling very stressed, and this might increase how intense their symptoms are. Also, if an individual tends to interpret their symptoms as warning signs, when in fact they are not, they may end up stopping doing things that might actually be helping. Equally, if someone tends to incorrectly interpret their symptoms anything other than warning signs, this might mean that they boom and bust and suffer more setbacks and relapses.

Definitions

Warning signs	*Recovery signs*	*Natural response*
These are symptoms that mean you are heading for a setback or relapse. It is your body's way of telling you that you need to do something.	These symptoms may not be pleasant, and may even be painful, but they do not result in a major setback. These symptoms are experienced as a sign that your body is reconditioning itself.	These symptoms are not pleasant either, and may even be quite anxiety-provoking, but they do not result in a major setback. These symptoms to some extent may be unrelated to your CFS/ME, or indirectly related to you CFS/ME because of the way your CFS/ME has affected you and your behaviour.

It is important to note again that for each individual the meaning and consequence of symptoms may be different. The table below is an example of what the consequences of a symptom might mean for an imaginary individual—**it may not be true for you.**

Situation	Feeling flu-like symptoms when you have been overdoing things	Been shopping for 20 minutes	Watching a film for the first time in a while after not sleeping the night before.
Symptoms	Flu-like symptoms and tender glands	Muscular aches and pains	Brain-fog
Symptom map	Warning sign	Recovery sign	Natural response
What your body is trying to say	You have been over-doing things. Try to pace yourself more in future.	Your body is getting fitter, and the more you gradually increase this activity into your life, the less aches and pains you will experience.	This is a natural response to the situation. Better sleep and gradu-ally building up your concentration levels may, over time, reduce this symptom.
Conse-quences of ignoring the message from the body	If you do not slow down, you experience a setback.	If you stop the activity alto-gether, your body does not get fitter	Your CFS/ME does not greatly worsen, but unless you get better sleep and build-up your concentration levels, this symp-tom is unlikely to improve.

What to do if you experience a warning sign symptom

A warning sign symptom does not necessarily mean stop all activity. It may seem counterintuitive, but identifying a warning sign symptom can be very helpful. It may be helpful if you respond to a warning sign by taking the following steps:

- Identify the behaviour that led to the warning sign.
- Reduce this behaviour so it does not lead you to crashing.
- Repeat the behaviour at the new reduced level, and gradually increase it over time.

Symptom mapping

People with CFS/ME often experience a bewildering array of symptoms, and this makes it very difficult to work out what each of your symptoms mean and what the consequence of your symptoms are. Additionally, the consequence of your symptoms may be different in different situations. Because of this complexity, you may find it helpful to employ a systematic approach to help you figure out the meaning and consequences of your symptoms. Symptom mapping is about working out what each of your symptoms mean for you, and may help you to work out how best to respond to them.

Symptom mapping asks you to note down what you are predicting about your symptom, and to use this thought to generate an impact cross. This might help you to figure out if your thoughts and behaviour are increasing the intensity of your symptom. We want to emphasise again that we are not saying that your symptoms are 'all in your head'. Instead, we are suggesting that how we think about a symptom affects how we experience it, and our behaviour affects how we cope with it.

Example symptom map

Symptom	Situation	What do you think will happen?
Brain fog	Trying to read the morning newspaper.	I will crash and be bedridden. It will set me back 1 year.

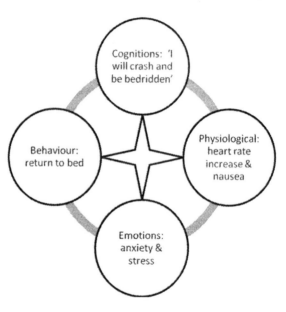

What was the consequence of the symptom?

I felt tired and drained, and quite stressed because I was worried about crashing. However, I did not actually crash.

Was it a warning sign, a recovery sign or a natural response?

Natural response.

How shall I deal with the symptom in future?

In future, I know that I do not need to worry about this symptom as it did not lead me to crashing.

Perhaps, I need to slowly build-up my concentration levels, as I am not used to focussing for long periods of time.

After you have completed your own symptom map, ask yourself whether your thought about your symptom increased how stressed you felt? Did this have an impact on how intense you experienced your symptom? Have you noticed a relationship between how stressed you feel and the severity and duration of your symptoms? If this is case, you could try either taking your thought about your symptom 'to court', or even taking an iTEST on your symptom.

Also take notice of how you respond to the symptom. Did you respond to a 'warning sign' symptom by trying to push yourself through? Did you respond to a 'natural response' symptom by stopping all activity? Using what you have learnt through reading this book, decide whether your behavioural responses to your symptom are making things worse or making things better. This may mean that you have to experiment with different responses to different symptoms until you find one that helps you the most. We hope that symptom mapping will help you to do this.

Blank symptom map

Symptom	Situation	What do you think will happen?

Cognition:

Behaviour:

Physiological:

Emotions:

What was the consequence of the symptom?

Was it a warning sign, a recovery sign or a natural response?

How shall I deal with the symptom in future?

CHAPTER TWELVE

Planning for setbacks

Setbacks are a normal part of any recovery. After working through this book and implementing the strategies and tools within, you may find that things are going well for a while, and then, all of a sudden, you experience an intensification of your symptoms. This is not your body telling you to throw away this book. Nor does it mean that you have taken one step forward and several steps back. By working through this book, we hope that you have learnt some useful techniques that will have benefited you. If you do experience a setback, it is to these strategies and tools that we advise you to turn.

In fact, we would suggest that you make a plan for setbacks and relapses before they happen. It is much more difficult to work out how to deal with a setback when you are experiencing one, than when you are feeling well. Having a solid setback plan can help you shorten the duration of the flare-up of your symptoms. Remember, by working your way through this book you have furnished yourself with strategies and tools and, hopefully, you have developed a greater understanding of your CFS/ME. You are in a better position now to deal with any setback than you were before you picked up this book.

The very first thing to remember if and when you experience a setback is not to panic. It is likely that you have noticed yourself the effect of anxiety and stress on your symptoms. Anxiety and stress-provoking thoughts like '*I will never get better*' or '*I am right back to square one*' need to be challenged, and now you can take the iTEST to help you do this.

Distinguishing between a CFS/ME and a non-CFS/ME setback

In order to plan what to do, you need to figure out whether you are experiencing a CFS/ME or a non-CFS/ME setback. A CFS/ME setback is a major intensification of your symptoms due to CFS/ME, and a non-CFS/ME setback is due to everything and anything else. It is helpful to plan to treat CFS/ME setback differently than you would a non-CFS/ME setback.

Breaking your leg or straining a muscle in your back would be, quite obviously, a non-CFS/ME setback. However, more often than not, distinguishing a CFS/ME from a non-CFS/ME setback is not going to be so straightforward. For example, for many people, there is a great deal of overlap between the symptoms of CFS/ME and the symptoms of flu. Both can leave you feeling fatigued, awash with aches and pains, and with a general sense of malaise. However, we suggest that you respond to flu in a different way altogether than a CFS/ME setback. Flu would be best addressed by taking plenty of fluids and lots of bed rest. A CFS/ME setback would require a different approach—for example, we would not recommend stopping all activity because of the physiological risk associated with such a response.

Despite the overlap between the symptoms of CFS/ME and those of a cold or the flu, there are some characteristics that might help you distinguish between the two. For example, some people report feeling hot when they have a CFS/ME setback, and it is common for people who have caught colds or the flu to have raised temperatures. However, if you have caught a cold or the flu, your core body temperature is likely to be high. This can be measured using a thermometer. It is not common for people who have a CFS/ME setback to have a raised core body temperature, even though they may feel hot. Also, runny noses and excess mucus tend to common in colds and flu, but not in CFS/ME relapses. Below is a table that might help you distinguish between a CFS/ME and a non-CFS/ME setback. It lists those symptoms that are commonly associated with CFS/ME and non-CFS/ME setbacks.

Symptoms	CFS/ME setback	Non-CFS/ME setback
Feeling hot	☑	☑
Raised core temperature	☒	☑
Aches and pains	☑	☑
Feeling fatigue	☑	☑
General sense of malaise	☑	☑
Excess mucus	☒	☑
Nausea	☒	☑
Coughing	☒	☑

It is important that if your setback has a new symptom that you have not experienced before, you seek advice from a doctor.

So, let's imagine that you have figured out that you are experiencing a CFS/ME setback. What do you do next? The next step is to figure out the cause or causes of your setback. Understanding the trigger or triggers for your setback may help reduce your stress levels, and might help you avoid or cope better with the causes in future. In order to work out what the cause or causes were of your setback, we would advise you to use some of the tools that we have discussed in this book.

Possible contributing factors to a CFS/ME relapse

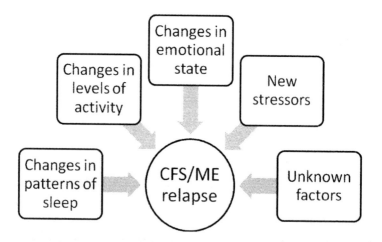

Clearly, by their very nature, you will not be able to identify the unknown factors that may contribute to your setback; however, by using some of the tools presented in this book, you may be able to identify other factors that might be contributing to your relapse. How you respond to a CFS/ME relapse is likely to affect the duration and intensity of the setback.

Changes in patterns of sleep

If your sleep pattern has become disrupted, then this may, in part, contribute to an escalation of your CFS/ME symptoms. You could try using the sleep diaries presented in Chapter 4 to monitor your sleep pattern. Perhaps you could try working through Chapter 4 to help you establish a stable pattern of sleep.

Changes in levels of activity

Has there been an increase in the demands placed on you? Sometimes sudden increases in activity are unavoidable. You may have had to help organize and attend your daughter's wedding, or take care of a partner when they have become ill. Other times, an increase on the demands placed on you seems more unavoidable than they actually are. Either way, completing some activity diaries from Chapter 5 may help you identify any unhelpful patterns of activity. Perhaps working through Chapters 5 and 6 might help to re-establish your activity baseline, and manage you energy levels more efficiently.

Changes in emotional state

Our emotional state can impact on our physical wellbeing. Have you been feeling unhappy lately? Can you identify what it was that has made you feel this way? What thoughts are going through your mind when you are feeling low? You could use the thoughts and feelings diary to identify what thoughts are troubling you. You could also try using the iTest (described in Chapter 8) to address problematic negative thoughts.

New stressors

Have you experienced any stressful events in your life recently? They may have occurred a few weeks back before the onset of your relapse. Try to identify what the stressful event or events are or were. Are they ongoing stressors? Work through the chapter on stress and anxiety (Chapter 9) to see if it provides you with any ideas of how you might deal with stressors.

CHAPTER THIRTEEN

Medical perspective

Advances in technology have touched many areas of our lives, from microwave ovens to mobile phones and the field of medicine is no exception. Consequently our theoretical understanding of fatigue has been enhanced. The exact process by which fatigue occurs however, and the way in which genetic and environmental factors might influence such a process, has yet to be emphatically elucidated. This remains the aim of ongoing research which will hopefully bring closer the definitive approach to prevention, treatment and cure of chronic and debilitating fatigue.

The preceding chapters have outlined the cognitive behavioural approach to dealing with fatigue and the other symptoms that occur with it in CFS/ME. In the early chapters we broached the commonly expressed concern about the use of CBT as a treatment for CFS/ME. In this chapter our intention is to consider the theoretical possibilities and the existing scientific and medical evidence for whether fatigue has a physical cause or a psychological cause, or both, and so illustrate how and why CBT may be helpful in addressing the chronicity of fatigue, whatever the cause.

Fatigue as protective mechanism?

It is common knowledge that an illness such as the common cold may be associated with fatigue; we know too that fatigue occurs with many other illnesses, to a greater or lesser degree, often varying with the severity of the illness. An obvious question therefore is whether there is a purpose to this fatigue? Could it be that being fatigued acts as a defence mechanism, facilitated by the immune system and its interaction with other body systems?

During an illness caused by infection, for example, in order to promote our recovery we develop a higher body temperature to prevent micro-organisms such as viruses and bacteria (that prefer lower temperatures) from replicating in our bodies. For the same reason, the levels of iron available in the blood decrease, as iron would help the micro-organisms to bind to human tissue, and cause more damage. Both these mechanisms would appear to be protective therefore. Similarly, fatigue develops during an illness to encourage us to rest and recover, and our appetite diminishes as well, the theory being that in the olden days fatigue and poor appetite would prevent us from venturing forth to forage for food in a less than fit state, which would make us less likely to survive attacks from predators! There are of course more evolved equivalents of these examples of the so-called adaptive mechanisms that allow us to overcome an illness and recover effectively, and safely. It might be useful at this point to remember the example of Vincent in Chapter 1.

Fatigue as a maladaptive mechanism?

Vincent ignored his symptoms, and also the stress induced by his drive to meet his own expectations. He did not take heed of the need to nurture himself and recover; unsurprisingly at this point his body/mind balance became unstable, the fatigue did not resolve when the trigger (for example, the infecting organism) had resolved, and his other symptoms persisted, and yet new symptoms developed.

It should have been at this point that Vincent, and indeed most people, books a visit to the doctor. It is likely that the doctor would perform a series of blood tests and an examination to exclude those illnesses which are reflected in blood abnormalities or physical findings such as rashes, or lumps and bumps.

Once the long list of possible causes for fatigue has been considered and the doctor finds that none of these causes apply, the fatigue and its associated symptoms are said to be unexplained, hence the term 'Medically Unexplained Symptoms' (MUS) (see pages 130 & 131). Since we know that short term fatigue may be explained as an adaptive (good) initial response to recovery, recent research has concentrated on establishing whether the unexplained and chronic fatigue and associated symptoms are a maladaptive (bad) response to recovery.

Joined up Government?

First we will outline the role of the various systems in the body that interact under normal circumstances to maintain equilibrium and health and we will follow this with results of some studies that show how they come to interact in a dysfunctional way and how we believe this may result in the symptoms of CFS/ME.

The diagram on page 126 appears complicated, but we shall try to explain it over the next few pages.

The central nervous system is made up of the brain and spinal cord. The brain houses an area called the limbic system which is the powerhouse of the emotions, such as pleasure, happiness, fear and anger, all of which influence our *psycho*logical state.

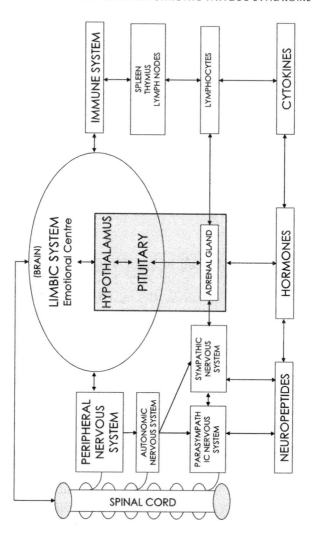

The limbic system recognises physical or psychological threats to life and modifies behaviour towards safety. It communicates directly with the hypothalamus (H), which sits at the base of the brain and in turn communicates directly with the pituitary (P) gland below it, which in turn stimulates the adrenal (A)

gland. The HPA axis produces hormones that act as *chemical messengers.*

The peripheral nervous system is comprised of nerve fibres emanating from the spinal cord that carry information to different parts of the body including the extremities (hence peripheral) and back along the nerve fibres to the spinal cord and hence to the brain for processing. Nerve fibre endings produce *neuro*peptides that act as *chemical messengers.*

The autonomic nervous system is made of two parts that are known as the sympathetic nervous system and the parasympathetic nervous system the nerve fibres of which supply the same organs but with opposite effects and usually act to balance each other by producing corresponding levels of *chemical messengers.*

Immunology is the science behind the defence force of the body. The immune system is comprised of organs such as the spleen and thymus gland, and lymph nodes and cells such as lymphocytes, which produce cytokines that act as *chemical messengers.*

Psycho-neuro-immunology

This all adds up to psychoneuroimmunology (PNI), a term of which you may have heard, although it is a relatively new area of research. The diagram and the outline above give a hint of the complexity of these multidirectional interactions under normal circumstances. In the case of medically unexplained symptoms (MUS) PNI looks at how physical (e.g. infection) and emotional (e.g. overwork, burnout, bereavement) stressors might affect the interactions between the brain, the nerve fibres and the immune system. As the term seems long and complicated, indeed the interactions are also complicated, which is why it has been difficult to outline the process from adaptive to maladaptive response.

Excessive stressors on the body and/or mind may result in imbalances of chemical messengers. As you can see from the diagram, all these chemical messengers communicate with each other and the brain and other organs, and an imbalance in one may cause an imbalance in the others with consequent knock on effects.

One theory is that the immune system, and specifically the lymphocytes, becomes persistently activated. This results in intermittent increases in cytokine levels and other cells that measure the level of lymphocyte activation known as markers.

Findings from various studies have shown the following:

- In CFS/ME patients, levels of these markers have been associated with disturbed sleep, impairment of memory and decreased concentration, headaches, and tender lymph nodes (see criteria below). It was also shown from this study that the degree of immune activation is associated with the severity of the CFS/ME symptoms.
- Cytokine abnormalities may impact on the balance between the sympathetic and parasympathetic nervous systems causing dry mouth, fast heart rate, muscle fatigue and mood changes.
- Increases in certain cytokine levels may result in a maladaptive stress response. Cytokines may interact with the HPA axis and may result in CFS/ME symptoms such as temperature fluctuation and muscle and joint pain. The HPA may communicate this to the limbic system and increase anxiety.
- HPA axis imbalance is responsible for sleeplessness and certain cytokines may induce sleepiness. Cytokines may decrease REM sleep, and also disrupt stages 3 and 4 of sleep (see Chapter 4).
- The brain receives feedback from the HPA and the immune system. Any imbalance in the HPA, for example, a decrease in

cortisol such as is found in some CFS/ME patients, may result in an increase in cytokines. Again, the brain may interpret these abnormalities as stressors and so the cycle continues.

In addition it is postulated that once the cycle of imbalance has occurred, it requires a much lower level of imbalance in any of the systems to perpetuate the cycle further. In other words all the systems have become sensitized.

The brain and body may have become primed to have the same maladaptive response to any stressor and that maladaptive response has become a conditioned (learned) response.

We should emphasise that these findings inform the theories as to how and why fatigue may be mediated. Further research is needed to establish the exact mechanism and therefore a model of illness that will explain the unexplained rather than the theory. This is no easy task, and as we have illustrated, there are probably several different pathways leading to the end result of the patient with severe fatigue and associated symptoms.

In the meantime, the science is all very well. But how do we identify those who have CFS/ME? Many people exhibit different symptoms with differing severity and in order to be able to formulate a diagnosis, we need to explain how using scientific and research tools including definitions, criteria and epidemiology may aid in approaching a diagnosis. This will also underpin our understanding of how common the illness is, and inform government policy about the provision of services.

Calling ME names?

First we will expand on the variety of names that have been used to describe what we now call Chronic Fatigue Syndrome/ Myalgic Encephalomyelitis (CFS/ME) and are outlined in the box on page 130.

Explaining names

(In alphabetical order)

Chronic Fatigue Syndrome (CFS)	In this term the word chronic refers to the persistent and ongoing presence of the major symptom, fatigue. A syndrome refers to a group of symptoms which consistently occur together and in this instance may include sore or painful muscles and/or joints, tender lymph nodes, headaches, deterioration in short term memory and concentration span, and unrefreshing sleep.
Chronic Fatigue and Immune Dysfunction Syndrome (CFIDS)	This term is most used in America. Given that the pattern of immune dysfunction and its role in causation of symptoms has not yet been fully elucidated, we are not using this term here.
Medically Unexplained Symptoms (MUS)	Symptoms for which there is no physical or laboratory correlation. There are a number of illnesses which fall into this category, for example, fibromyalgia and other pain syndromes such as atypical chest pain.
Myalgic Encephalomyelitis (ME)	This term describes an illness that occurred in the medical staff at the Royal Free Hospital in 1955. The symptoms included myalgia, which means muscle pain, and which was

	accompanied by clinical evidence that the brain (encephalo-) and spinal cord (myelo-) were inflamed (-itis). Most patients with CFS have myalgia but do not exhibit the inflammation of the brain and spinal cord. ME is however a term in common usage and has been used interchangeably with CFS by some and for some time. The Chief Medical Officer in the report of 2002 suggested that the all encompassing term of **CFS/ME** be used.
Post Viral Fatigue Syndrome (PVFS)	The virus classically implicated here is Epstein-Barr virus (EBV). EBV is responsible for glandular fever (also known as infectious mononucleosis, the latter being a description of findings on a blood test) and may result in fatigue even after the virus has left the body, but this fatigue usually resolves within six months. Other viral infections may follow a similar pattern, as indeed may other illnesses not caused by viruses.

Criteria

We will use criteria to define CFS/ME. Some believe that such criteria are based on research and can at best only be descriptive. Everyone agrees that the most important point is to describe and quantify the fatigue, which is the major disabling symptom and differentiates CFS/ME from the condition of fibromyalgia and other pain syndromes.

In 1988 the first criteria for CFS/ME were outlined and have subsequently been refined on several occasions as more information about the condition has been gathered. The two sets of criteria in most common use in the United Kingdom are the Oxford Criteria and the Centers for Disease Control (CDC) criteria, which are outlined in the boxes on pages 132 and 133.

Sometimes, some patients do not have a full house of criteria, and some find symptoms other than the fatigue more debilitating, for example, disturbed sleep. This does not mean that a diagnosis of CFS/ME cannot be made, as long as the fatigue as described is present.

Other patients may report disordered bowel function as a significant problem. Again, this will not refute a diagnosis of CFS/ME, as long as the bowel dysfunction has been investigated and conditions such as celiac disease excluded. Bowel dysfunction may be due to Irritable Bowel Syndrome (IBS) and this may co-exist with CFS/ME, without altering either diagnosis.

Oxford criteria

- Fatigue is the principal symptom, and it has a definite onset, in other words it has not been a lifelong complaint.
- Fatigue should have been present for at least six months and should be present for at least fifty percent of the time.
- The fatigue is severe and disabling, and affects both physical and mental functioning, and is disproportionate to exertion.
- A constellation of other symptoms may be present and include myalgia (sore or painful muscles), sleep disturbance and diminished short term memory and concentration span.

Centers for Disease Control (CDC) criteria

The definition CDC criteria are a little more specific and suggest that apart from the fatigue, four or more of the following symptoms are present for at least six months:

- Impaired memory or concentration
- Sore throat
- Tender cervical (neck) or axilliary (armpit) lymph nodes
- Muscle ache/pain
- Multijoint ache or pain
- New type of headaches
- Unrefreshing sleep
- Postexertional malaise (feeling ill)

Who gets CFS/ME?

Epidemiology is the study of the pattern of a particular condition in the population. It takes account of the number of new cases (incidence) and the total number of cases in existence (prevalence) at any one time in a particular place.

It therefore allows us to see who gets CFS/ME and hence we know that while male and female patients of a wide age range may acquire the condition, it is most common in women in their late thirties. This led us to think that there might be an auto-immune cause to the illness, as auto-immune illnesses are more common in women and there is a peak at the same age. This theory has not been validated. CFS/ME may occur at almost any age and in most ethnic groups. It is clear however that there are different patterns in the way the illness might evolve for different people; indeed, it might be that there are different variants, known as sub-groups of CFS/ME. It terms of diagnosis therefore, defining criteria are helpful for doctors and patients. And so it might be with genomics.

Is CFS/ME hereditary?

Genomics is the study of the genetic material in all cells of a living organism, and that includes human beings. Specific studies, including those done in twins, have shown it is possible that CFS/ME may run in families. Criticism of such studies done so far have been that the numbers of people in the studies have been too small and the results too variable to make a significant conclusion.

Nonetheless, some of the information from earlier studies has been regarded as important. Larger studies are being conducted to expand on the findings that have suggested the genes governing the immune and nervous systems may result in a predisposition to CFS/ME. This is not to say that we are born with CFS/ME, but it may be likely that any genetically influenced abnormality increases the susceptibility, rather than being the trigger itself, for developing CFS/ME. It might be that this abnormality decreases the threshold of the various body systems to respond to exposure to physical, psychological, emotional or environmental triggers.

To repeat the question, why CBT?

At the beginning of this book we explained why CBT could be used to treat CFS/ME. Throughout the book and in this chapter we have described a model of illness that incorporates the physiological, psychological and environmental as potential triggers and maintaining factors in CFS/ME. If indeed the maladaptive response is a conditioned response that ultimately results in a deconditioned state of mind and body, the tools and techniques of CBT should aid in reconditioning and recovery.

Some practicalities

If you believe that you may have developed CFS/ME, the sensible approach is to register with a doctor who is likely to refer you to a specialist service dedicated to CFS/ME and its treatment.

For many it is a significant relief just to have their condition diagnosed. We appreciate this, but also believe that a collaborative process between patient and health professional will go a long way to furthering the recovery process, and help to prevent the relapsing aspect of this distressing condition. Certain symptoms, such as pain and headaches may also be treated with medication, and again we emphasise that such decisions are made by the patient in conjunction with the health professional. We also recommend the consideration of other therapies such as Graded Exercise Therapy and Adaptive Pacing Therapy, both of which patients may find helpful, and sometimes preferable. It is also possible to have a multidisciplinary approach, with input from different therapists, specially trained in collaborating with patients with CFS/ME.

Above all, we believe it is essential that those diagnosed with CFS/ME have access to specialist services where they, and their family and friends, may make informed choices about their road to recovery.